MOZART AND LEADBELLY

Ernest J. Gaines was born on a plantation in
Pointe Coupee Parish near New Roads, Louisiana,
which is the Bayonne of all his fictional works. He
is writer-in-residence emeritus at the University of
Louisiana at Lafayette. In 1993 Gaines received
the John D. and Catherine T. MacArthur Founda-
tion Fellowship for his lifetime achievements. In
1996 he was named Chevalier de l'Ordre des Arts
et des Lettres, one of France's highest decorations.
He and his wife, Dianne, live in Oscar, Louisiana.

MOZART AND LEADBELLY

Mozart and Leadbelly

Stories and Essays

Ernest J. Gaines

Compiled and edited by
Marcia Gaudet and Reggie Young

Vintage Contemporaries
Vintage Books
A Division of Random House, Inc.
New York

FIRST VINTAGE CONTEMPORARIES EDITION, OCTOBER 2006

The following were originally published in earlier versions as listed: "Miss Jane and I,"
Callaloo, 1978; "Mozart and Leadbelly," *Phi Kappa Phi National Forum*, 1998; "A Very
Big Order: Reconstructing Identity," *Southern Review*, 1990, and Louisiana Endowment
for the Humanities, *Louisiana Cultural Vistas*, 1990 (published simultaneously);
"Bloodline in Ink," *CEA Critic*, 1989, and *Georgia Review*, 1989; "Aunty and the Black
Experience in Louisiana," *Louisiana Tapestry*, 1982; "The Turtles," *Transfer*, 1956; "Boy
in the Double-Breasted Suit," *Transfer*, 1957; "Mary Louise," *Stanford Short Stories*,
1960; "My Grandpa and the Haint," *New Mexico Quarterly*, 1966; "Oyster/Shrimp
Po'boys, Chardonnay, and Conversation with Ernest Gaines," *Interdisciplinary
Humanities*, 2002, published as "The Influence of Multi-Art Forms on the Artist."

The Library of Congress has cataloged the Knopf edition as follows:
Gaines, Ernest J., 1933–
Mozart and Leadbelly : stories and essays / Ernest J. Gaines. —1st ed.
p. cm.
1. Louisiana—Social life and customs—Fiction. 2. Gaines, Ernest J., 1933–
—Childhood and youth. 3. Authors, American—20th century—Biography.
4. African American authors—Biography. 5. African Americans—Fiction.
6. California—Biography. 7. Louisiana—Biography. I. Title.
PS3557.A355M697 2005
818'.5409—dc22
2004063264

Vintage ISBN-10: 1-4000-9645-6
Vintage ISBN-13: 978-1-4000-9645-9

Book design by Anthea Lingeman

www.vintagebooks.com

Printed in the United States of America
10   9   8   7   6   5   4   3   2   1

To my brothers and sisters
and in memory of
my mother, Adrean Jefferson Colar

CONTENTS

INTRODUCTION

I think the artist must deal with both God and the Devil. I think you can't put one aside or the other. You know, if you're going to write for certain groups, and I don't believe in writing for any specific group. So let others call blues the "sin music" and gospel is God's music. . . . But the artist himself cannot separate the religious or the blues or the spiritual. The artist cannot.

ERNEST J. GAINES

When this book was still in its embryonic stages, we made the first of several trips from our campus in Lafayette to False River to discuss the project with the man we know better as "Ernie." Both Dianne (Mrs. Gaines, who might be the only person in his circle of family members and friends who calls him Ernest—his old "homeboys" have always called him E. J.) and Ernie had recently finished consolidating several households they had maintained through the years in different cities around the country—including Lafayette, New Orleans, Miami, and San Francisco—into *"La maison entre les champs et la rivière,"* a name given to the newly built Gaines residence by Ernie's longtime booking agent Tanya Bickley. The house sits on the land of the same plantation where Ernie was born and spent the early years of his life. It is the same plantation landscape where most of the stories in the Ernest J. Gaines fictional universe are set.

Both of us had visited Ernie and Dianne at the camp they still maintain on the river—which is actually an oxbow lake, across the road from the new house—one that consists of a trailer home and a deck that extends out into the river. In previous years, the Gaineses usually spent the week in their Lafayette home near the university where Ernie has served as writer-in-residence for the last two decades, and their weekends at the False River camp. (He is now in semiretirement, but his appointment at the university is one that he holds for life.) We had seen their new house during various stages of its construction, but for both of us this was our first visit after the Gaineses had moved in. Our purpose for coming, however, was not strictly social. We had been in discussion with Ernie over the summer about one of several projects dedicated both to commemorate his upcoming retirement from the University of Louisiana at Lafayette and to pay homage to a remarkable career as a writer that promises to extend itself well into the future. This book was one of those ideas.

In the beginning, we conceived this book as something that would be published by our own Center for Louisiana Studies, a program at the university that devotes itself primarily to the scholarly concerns of the region. The book would have served two purposes: to give exposure to the center as a growing and developing university press, and to make available to the scholarly community various writings (some composed as talks) that were either unavailable or difficult to find. Since Ernie wholeheartedly supports the university and its efforts, he was more than happy to allow it to place in print these works, which he assumed would have little value to anyone other than the kind of scholars who like to "pick over everything" that a writer has ever done.

It is important to point out that Ernie was not really enthusiastic about our idea to compile all of his "old and dusty writings" together in a collection. If anyone else had approached him with the idea (and at least one person had in the past), chances are he would have laughed and sent that person away empty-handed. For a lot of people, he would not have even bothered with the laugh. But he likes the two of us and he also likes the center, and anyone who knows Ernest Gaines very well will realize the possibility that the permission he gave us to publish his works might well have been a retirement present to us. He's just that kind of man. Maybe he was feeling sorry for the two of us because of the many years to come before we will be able to join him at our leisure, day after day, fishing in False River or sitting in one of the rockers on the porch of *la maison* Gaines, chewing cane and discussing the books and writers that serve as our common passion. Knowing Ernie, he probably felt it was the least he could do because we still have to read student papers night after night and direct dissertations, while he does not.

During this meeting, three important things happened. The first was that Ernie told us he felt an obligation to run the material by his literary agent, Jeff Gerecke. He said that Jeff might want to have Ash Green, his editor at Knopf, look at the material before making a commitment to the center. Since Knopf is his publisher, he didn't feel it would be right to have works he had written come out under the banner of a different publisher. At the time, none of us thought Knopf would have interest in the various pieces; after all, they had been around and available to Knopf for years. The most we hoped for was that Knopf might agree to publish the works jointly with the Center for Louisiana Studies as a favor to Ernie because of their long-standing relationship. But we were wrong. As soon as Ash Green received the material—various pieces that had been scanned from different sources and that had not yet been typed into a manuscript—he began editing the works for publication. There was no deliberation on his part; he knew these works deserved widespread circulation.

The second thing that happened involves the story that opens the book's second section: "Christ Walked Down Market Street." We had heard Ernie, during previous discussions, tell how—*in his opinion*—all the stories he had tried to write that were set away from Louisiana were failures. In fact, he has stated this publicly in talks such as one titled "Miss Jane and I," which is the opening essay in this volume. But as we drove along La. 190 that day on our way to *la maison* Gaines on False River, we wondered if we needed to look at these works that Ernie has always dismissed. We had little faith in Ernie as a judge of his own work. Most of his efforts that he views as failures would make a lesser writer's career. Then we remembered this particular story that Ernie had read once at our Deep South Festival of Writers and one that he had mentioned to us as his personal favorite of everything he had ever written. We thought, why not include "Christ Walked Down Market Street" in this collection?

This is a story Ernie wrote while serving a semester as a visiting writer at the University of Houston's downtown campus twenty years ago, and it involves his desire to write a story with a title similar to one he had read by Nobel laureate Isaac Bashevis Singer titled "The Spinoza of Market Street." But having spent so much time on Market Street in San Francisco, Ernie wanted to use that city as the setting for his work. Without giving away the story's plot, we feel it is important to point out that he wrote it out in longhand, as he still does the first drafts of everything he writes, and then typed it after he returned to the Bay area. Other than his reading the story at our Deep South "festival" and on one other occasion, the story served no purpose other than to sit in a private spot among his other possessions. But he had always insisted that out of everything he had written, this was his favorite story. We thought that alone made it a crucial piece to have as part of our collection. He agreed to consider our request and went to retrieve his only copy of the story—only one other copy of this work existed at the time in Ernie's papers at UL Lafayette's Dupré Library in files that are unavailable to the general public. When he came back just a minute or two later, he held in his hand a group of rolled-up goldenrod sheets of paper with a rubber band around them. He sat down and with a kind of jovial look on his face told us again about the circumstances behind the story's composition, which would make a great essay for any future collections like this one. Then he began reading from the sheets, including the story's introduction (which also introduces the story in this book), and as he read, his face lit up like a Christmas tree in July. The two of us sat there in awe of the personal reading we were receiving from someone who is in constant demand from colleges, universities, and arts organizations to read his works before large audiences—from a writer who has been honored with numerous literary awards and whose works have been translated into at least a dozen different languages. It seemed as if he decided right then that our book idea was a good one and that he would let us include "Christ Walked Down Market Street" because his love for it alone made it worthy of publication.

The third thing that happened that day was Ernie also agreed to let us include a talk that he had been giving at recent speaking engagements, "Writing *A Lesson Before Dying*." He had explained his reluctance by saying, "If I let you guys put that talk in print, then I won't have anything people haven't read the next time I'm asked to come and speak." We felt that placing it in print would actually increase its value as a stump speech while he works away on what we hope will one day develop into his next novel, *The Man Who Whipped Children*. Reading and hearing are two different experiences, and when Ernie has presented his *Lesson* talk, he has always added off-the-cuff remarks to the prepared text to further explain things in more detail, to offer illustrations about people or events he mentioned, or to offer humorous anecdotes. In fact, his spirited and informative question-and-answer sessions where he often engages audiences in lively discussions are alone reason enough to attend his events. We argued that people often like writers to read material they already possess, because it allows them to read the words off the page while they hear them in the author's voice and from the author's mouth. There are thousands of readers across the country and around the world who will have the opportunity to discover this talk on the printed page who may never have a chance to hear him read it. Besides, we argued, if "Christ Walked Down Market Street" was included in the volume, it would become another piece that audiences all over would enjoy hearing him read.

For those familiar with Gaines's works, whether scholars, students, or general readers, this volume will be a welcome edition because it illustrates his development as a writer and offers illumination into the process that has resulted in the masterworks of the Gaines canon: *Catherine Carmier* (his first published novel and one deserving of a renaissance), *Of Love and Dust* (which is still considered by a select few to be his best), *Bloodline* (the story collection that includes such favorites as "The Sky Is Gray," "Just Like a Tree," and "A Long Day in November"), *The Autobiography of Miss Jane Pittman* (one of the most important of all twentieth-century novels and a work that is so successful in portraying the female voice that unknowledgeable readers still mistakenly think it was actually written by a woman named Jane Pittman), *In My Father's House* (the only Ernest Gaines novel that explores the relationship between fathers and sons), *A Gathering of Old Men* (one of the most revealing testaments ever written on the strength of human dignity), and *A Lesson Before Dying* (a work that became an instant classic and that has been the subject of programs such as the Seattle Reads Ernest J. Gaines's *A Lesson Before Dying*—it has already been adopted and read by dozens of cities across the country). For new readers who are encountering the writings of Ernest Gaines for the first time, this book will no doubt serve as an introduction to a writer whose success has made him the personification of what it means to be a national treasure.

The Ernest J. Gaines story is a familiar one to many, but new readers will learn more of his background from his own words in the essays that follow than we could hope to convey in this introduction. Still, it might be helpful to provide some background on the various stories and essays collected here.

The first section comprises talks Ernie has given over the years, and the dates of their initial presentations range from 1971 to 2001.

The fact that these essays were written as talks is something that Ernie felt important for readers to know, since they were not written with publication in mind. He emphasizes the fact that he is a writer of stories and not an essayist. There are some things he repeats from one essay to another, but this is not redundant writing; instead, it points out the consistency of his story and how it has influenced his developing vision as a writer. Since the talks were presented to different audiences over the years, what individuals in attendance heard when Ernie discussed being raised by an aunt who never walked a day in her life, leaving the plantation to continue his schooling in California with his mother and stepfather, his experiences at San Francisco State College and at Stanford, the factors that motivated him to return to Louisiana once he had established that his life would be dedicated to writing, and other developments that are important to his literary legacy were new revelations about a writer whose books had touched their lives. We have altered the material in some places to eliminate repetition, but in other places we left everything as it was originally written for the sake of continuity and to give readers the full essence of that particular work.

Although Ernie, as a writer, does not view these essays with the same significance that we, as scholars of his works, do, it is important to point out that no matter what their original purpose, these are great pieces of writing. In fact, the talks in this volume with the exception of "Writing *A Lesson Before Dying*," have appeared *as essays* in preeminent literary journals such as *Callaloo*, *Southern Review*, and *Georgia Review*, or have appeared in specialized publications that had small print runs, which means they received very little exposure. Now that they are available to a broader audience, each of the selections in this section will take on additional importance as a notable example of the personal essay. Without a doubt, the essays in this section will soon start appearing in leading literary anthologies as well as in textbooks for creative nonfiction classes.

Their value can be measured in terms of the volume's title and the theme that figuratively governs all of Gaines's work: *Mozart and Leadbelly.*

Years ago, in one of the essays from his collection *Shadow and Act*, Ralph Ellison said one cannot chose one's (racial and cultural) relatives, but one can choose one's own (literary and artistic) ancestors, and among the ones he chose were Hemingway, Eliot, Dostoyevsky, and Faulkner. It is interesting to see how Ellison's figurative concept of relatives and ancestors is revised by Gaines through the use of Mozart and Leadbelly as a metaphor for his own influences as a writer. His exposure to classical and canonical influences in literature, art, and music was important to his development as a writer in ways that are best explained by him in the essays that are to follow, but he does not privilege these over those of his own cultural heritage.

Gaines throughout his remarkable career has drawn equally from those we might now think of as his "ancestors," such as Mozart, Mussorgsky, and Turgenev, who provided examples of technique, form, beauty, and artistic excellence, *as well as* from relatives such as Big Bill Broonzy, Lightnin' Hopkins, and Bessie Smith, whose mastery of language allowed her to describe the Great Flood of 1927 in twelve lines of poetic blues lyrics, whereas it took Faulkner more than one hundred pages to do the same thing in prose. Even if Gaines did not have works of black writers to draw upon in his developmental period as a writer, he balanced the influence of the Mozart tradition with that of what we might think of as the blues culture of his youth, the cultural environment that permeated the plantation quarters where he spent many of his formative years and to which he returned to find his voice as a writer. In the title essay, "Mozart and Leadbelly," he relates a story he heard from a friend about a young black man on an elevator whistling a Mozart melody. Ernie makes it clear that whistling Mozart is a good thing, but also that "there is some value in whistling Bessie Smith or Leadbelly."

We are mindful of the fact that Ernest Gaines is a writer of novels and stories and that many readers will pick up this book primarily to encounter *new* Gaines stories. None of the stories in this collection are new in the sense of being newly written, but for most readers they will represent newly discovered treasures. For example, how many readers would cherish the opportunity to read the first story written by one of their favorite writers, especially if they knew the story was originally written in what we might think of as a desperate attempt to get a decent grade in a college composition course? In this volume is the story "The Turtles," Gaines's first published story, which in 1956 appeared in the first issue of *Transfer,* a literary magazine at San Francisco State that is still in publication today. At that time, Dorothea Oppenheimer was in the process of starting a literary agency. When she read this story she quickly enlisted Gaines as a client. The rest is history.

Besides "The Turtles" and the aforementioned "Christ Walked Down Market Street" are other stories that were published in magazines from earlier in Gaines's career, such as "My Grandpa and the Haint"—a story that so well embodies the language and themes that have become known as Ernest Gaines trademarks—the delightful "Boy in the Double-Breasted Suit," and "Mary Louise." Those familiar with Ernie's first novel, *Catherine Carmier,* may especially appreciate the fact that "Mary Louise" was an early draft of a work that eventually developed into that novel.

A recent critic proclaimed Ernest Gaines as the writer whose works best serve to extend the most important qualities of Southern literature, especially those of community and place. This might be true, but as much as any other American writer, Faulkner included, Gaines's writings grow out of a particular community and a particular place. Although students often tend to confuse the universal with the general or common, something we have all learned from James Joyce (as Grant Wiggins does in *A Lesson Before Dying*) is that the universal in art is always best captured through specific and particular depictions of human life. If the mantra of the Southern writer concerns the representation of community and place, Gaines can be best understood in terms of a particular land that habits a particular community of people, a land that is important to him because of the people—his people—who have inhabited it for generations, just as they do today. From reading the following essays, readers will discover that Gaines's apprenticeship as a writer was spent while serving as this community's scribe. Although he left the land, he never forgot his calling to serve. His service to these people as a writer illustrates that Gaines more so than any other writer in our history represents what it means to be an American griot.

Calling Gaines a griot is not at all far-fetched. But he is not African and has no pretensions about being one. His tales emanate from the plantation quarters where his ancestors endured slavery and Jim Crow, but his audience is primarily an American one and through America the rest of the world. His commitment to these people—*his people*—is demonstrated year in and year out in a ritualistic event that could easily be imagined as a scene in a Chinua Achebe novel or a depiction from Julie Dash's classic film *Daughters of the Dust* in the annual ceremony at the graveyard site where his ancestors, friends, and a brother are buried. Ernest and Dianne Gaines serve as president and vice president of the Mount Zion River Lake Cemetery Association in Cherie Quarters, Oscar, Louisiana, and in late October of each year, when pecans cover the cemetery grounds, shortly before All Saints' Day, they lead a gathering of family members and friends from all over the country, along with present and former students, in a special beautification ceremony dedicated to honoring the dead by cleaning their resting places and offering them a gift of communion from the living.

Those who have participated in this sacred event know a side of Gaines that is as important as anything he has ever written and that conveys the very spirit of his work as a storyteller. Anyone who has seen Gaines in such a setting is well aware that he is very spiritual. It is important not to confuse religion and spirituality in this instance, because people often act religiously by going through the motions without substance or real commitment. As with many of his most memorable characters, his spirituality is not limited to a specific day and hour of the week, and it is not confined to the dictates of fallible human institutions. As Gaines has said himself:

> My church is the oak tree. My church is the river. My church is walking right down the cane field road, on the headland between rows of sugarcane. That's my church. I can talk to God there as well as I can talk to him in Notre Dame. I think he's in one of those cane rows as much as he is in Notre Dame.

There is a particular church, however, that is of particular importance to Ernest Gaines's life. It is a church many of us have visited in scenes such as the one where young Jimmie is proclaimed to be "the One" in *The Autobiography of Miss Jane Pittman*, where Grant Wiggins teaches Irene Cole, and where Tante Lou and Miss Emma sing their Termination Songs in *A Lesson Before Dying*. A further illustration of his commitment to his people and the spirit of those who came before him on the land is his acquisition and restoration of the old church from the quarters where he grew up, the same church building where he attended Sunday services and completed the early years of his education. Today the church sits in back of *la maison entre les champs et la rivière*, next to the guesthouse that the Gaineses built on their property for the comfort of visiting family members and friends. Anyone who enters the church is struck by a solemn feeling not unlike that of being in the quarters' graveyard. It is as if it is a place where thousands through the generations have come for rest at the invitation of their griot, their storyteller and caretaker. The spirit of the church is the same spirit manifested in the pages of so many of Gaines's most notable works.

Gaines elaborates on this aspect of himself as a person and his writing in a recorded conversation between himself and Marcia Gaudet and Darrell Bourque that has been transcribed to serve as a closing coda to this book. Besides serving as coeditor of *Mozart and Leadbelly*, Marcia also served as an editor of one of the most widely read books of Ernest Gaines scholarship to date: the collection of interviews titled *Porch Talk with Ernest J. Gaines*. Both Marcia and Darrell have been close friends with Ernie through their years together as colleagues on the UL Lafayette English department faculty, and they are probably the only two people who could have engaged him in such a lively, open, and informal discussion. Of the published Ernest Gaines interviews, this one is among the best. It took place while the Gaineses still occupied the property that is now known as the Gaines House, the house just steps from the campus that was donated to the university by a local benefactor when Gaines agreed to come on board as writer-in-residence with the express purpose of allowing him to live there as long as he desired. The discussion that took place over the dining room table that day occurred as the participants broke bread together while consuming oyster/shrimp po'boys from Old Tyme Groceries (one of Ernie's favorite delicacies; in fact, if you ever plan to visit him, you would be wise to stop by Old Tyme in Lafayette to pick up some on the way), and libations from a vintage bottle of Chardonnay.

During their conversations, Gaines says a number of things that help to illustrate the importance of the Mozart and Leadbelly theme of this book. One in particular is a statement he makes about the use of the radio that Grant Wiggins gives to Jefferson in *A Lesson Before Dying*, one that Jefferson uses to listen to blues stations and that serves as an instrumental step in the process of the character reaching what we might think of as a secular salvation. Although some might see this term as an oxymoron, it is important to remember that Jefferson has been figuratively reduced by his own lawyer to the status of a hog, and any good Christian knows that Jesus Christ did not die to save such beasts. So when Gaines tells Marcia and Darrell that when Jefferson's in jail

> and he's playing that radio and he's listening to blues, the old man—the minister—says "that sin box." Well, sometimes that sin box can help you get to heaven as well as anything else. That's what I was trying to show. But the artist himself cannot separate the religious or the blues or the spiritual. The artist cannot.

Dichotomies such as the one that views the blues and spirituals as antithetical entities are nowhere to be found in Gaines's philosophy of art, and this is also true of his artistic influences. Therefore, in this interview he discusses such diverse sources of influence as Dvořák's *New World Symphony*, Mussorgsky's *Pictures at an Exhibition*, Lightnin' Hopkins singing "Tim Moore's Farm," and John Coltrane. For those who know Gaines only from a distance, the interview at the end of this book is an excellent opportunity to gain insight into the man while he is sitting back talking with friends as just Ernie.

It is our hope that this introduction will do more than preface the works that are to follow. It is from us, and especially from Ernie himself, a welcome to readers, new and old alike, to a collection of works that are like treasures from a vault that the world is being allowed to view for the first time. But unlike museum pieces, these are works you can actually hold on your own, experience at your leisure, and take with you to become part of your own valued possessions. We are both in anticipation of a new masterwork from Ernie in the future, one that many of us have been allowed to glimpse but that he does not want any of us to talk about. In the meantime, for those of us with an appetite for new and undiscovered works by Ernest J. Gaines, *Mozart and Leadbelly* promises to be as satisfying as any oyster/shrimp po'boy could ever be.

Marcia Gaudet and Reggie Young
University of Louisiana at Lafayette
December 15, 2004

Essays

Miss Jane and I

I shall try to say a little about myself, about my writing, and about Miss Jane Pittman and how she and I came to meet. Since the publication of *The Autobiography of Miss Jane Pittman*, I've read reviews in which critics have called Miss Jane a real person. A representative of *Newsweek* asked me to send the editors of the magazine a picture of Miss Jane Pittman to be used with a review of the novel. I had to inform her that I could not, since Miss Jane is a creation of my imagination. The lady who called me was both shocked and embarrassed—"Oh, my God! Oh, my God! Oh, my God!" she said. The actress Ruby Dee, when reviewing the novel for *Freedomways*, also mistook Miss Jane for a real person. Several newspapers made the same mistake. One lady accused me of using a tape recorder, then calling the interview a novel after I had cut out all the inconsequential material. A good friend of mine who writes for one of the leading newspapers in San Francisco felt that *Miss Jane* is definitely a novel, but he also felt that I must have, at some time in the past, interviewed my grandmother or my aunt who raised me when I lived in the South. Bob Cromie on *Bookbeat* out of Chicago also thought I had interviewed my grandmother.

But *The Autobiography of Miss Jane Pittman* is absolute fiction. By that I mean I created Miss Jane, and if I did not create all the events she mentions in her narrative, I definitely created all the situations that she is personally involved in.

It is written somewhere that when Gertrude Stein was dying, Alice B. Toklas leaned over her and asked, "Gertrude, Gertrude, what is the answer?" Gertrude Stein raised up on her dying bed and said, "Dear Alice, but what is the question?"

Who is Miss Jane Pittman? But first, who is Ernest J. Gaines? Because to get part of the answer to the former question we must go back, back, back—not to 1968, when I started writing the novel, but to 1948, when I had to leave the South.

Until I was fifteen years old, I had been raised by an aunt, a lady who had never walked a day in her life, but who crawled over the floor as a six-month-old child might. Some people have said that she had been dropped on the floor by another child when she was small; others have said that she was born with that affliction. To this day I do not know which story is true—but I've never met anyone who ever saw her walk.

When I say that my aunt raised me, I mean she did more than just look after me, my brothers, and my sister. I can remember us children bringing the potatoes, rice, meat, flour, and water to her sitting on her bench by the stove so that she could cook for us. I can remember the loaves of bread, cookies, and cakes she used to bake for us in the oven of the woodstove. I can remember seeing her sitting on her bench and leaning over a washboard, washing our clothes in a tin tub. Once this was done, and after she had taken her afternoon nap, she wanted to do more. She wanted to go into her garden then and chop grass from between the rows of beans, cabbages, and tomatoes. She had a small hoe, about half the size of the regular hoe. After sharpening it well with her file, she would let it down on the ground, and then in some way, but with true dignity, she would slide from step to step until she had reached the ground—then she would go into her garden. Other times she would go into the backyard with her little rice sack and gather pecans under the trees. No pecan, not even the smallest one, could hide itself in the bull grass from her eyes forever. They would try hard, the little pecans, but eventually they would give up the ghost just like all the rest. These are just a few of the things I can remember about my aunt, but there is much, much more.

Then there were the people who used to come to our house, because she was crippled and could not go to theirs. In summer they would sit out on the porch, the gallery—"the Garry," we called it—and they would talk for hours. There was no television then, and only a few people had radios, so people would talk. Sometimes there would be only one other person besides my aunt; other times, maybe a half dozen. Sometimes they would sew on quilts and mattresses while they talked; other times they would shell peas and beans while they talked. Sometimes they would just sit there smoking pipes, chewing pompee, or drinking coffee while they talked. I, being the oldest child, was made to stay close by and serve them coffee or water or whatever else they needed. In winter, they moved from the porch and sat beside the fireplace and drank coffee—and sometimes a little homemade brew—while they talked. But regardless of what time of year it was, under whatever conditions, they would find something to talk about. I did not know then that twenty or twenty-five years later I would try to put some of their talk in a book that I would title *The Autobiography of Miss Jane Pittman*.

This all took place before 1948. In 1948, I had to leave my aunt and the South to go West to my mother and stepfather to finish my education. I probably—I definitely—would have stayed in the South if I could have received the education that they thought I rightly deserved. But since there was no junior high or senior high school near me, and since I would have to go away to school anyhow, my mother and stepfather thought I should come to California, where they were. I remember the day I left. It was Sunday. It took me all day to pack, unpack, and repack the old brown leather suitcase. I didn't have many clothes, I can assure you, but for some reason I could not get it done. Maybe it was the bag of oranges, or the shoebox of fried chicken and bread, or the tea cakes and pralines wrapped in brown paper, or the bag of unshelled pecans—maybe it was one of these or all of these that kept me opening and shutting the suitcase. But, finally, I got it done and came out onto the porch. Everybody was there: the old people on the porch talking to my aunt and the children in the yard waiting for me to come down the steps so they could follow me to the road. I went to each one of the old people, shook their hands, and listened to their advice on how to live "up North." Then I went to my aunt. She sat on the floor—just inside the door. "I'm going, Aunty," I said. I did not lean over to kiss her— though I loved her more than I have loved anyone else in my life. I did not take her hand, as I had taken the other people's hands, because that would have been the most inappropriate thing in the world to do. I simply said, "I'm going, Aunty." She looked up at me from the floor. I saw the tears in her eyes. She nodded her head and looked down again. When I came out into the road, I looked back at her. I waved and smiled; she waved back. The old people were silent all this time—but I'm sure that before I reached the highway to catch the bus, they were talking again.

I went to Vallejo, California, a seaport town, because my stepfather was in the merchant marine. I had gone there in summer, and I had nothing much to do during the day but play with other children. We lived in the government projects at the time, and my friends were a complete mixture of races: Chinese, Japanese, Filipinos, Mexicans, Puerto Ricans, whites, and Indians. I made friends quite easily, and most of the time, especially during the day, I was very happy. But at night, when my new friends had gone, I sat alone in a room and thought about home. Many times I wished that my aunt would write my mother and tell her to send me back—or that some wise man would come up and tell me how futile an education was when I had to sacrifice so much for it.

A few months after I had gone to Vallejo, my parents moved out of the projects into another part of town. I did not have nearly as many friends there, and my stepfather warned me against those young people I did meet. They were a rough bunch, and he felt that they would all end up in jail before they graduated from high school. I took his advice about staying away from them, and that's how I found myself in the public library.

I soon found out that all I needed was a library card and then I could take out as many books as I could carry in my arms. At first I took books indiscriminately—I would choose one simply because I liked its dust jacket. But soon, because of the schoolwork, or maybe because of the weight of the books, I began to select only those that I would definitely read. Number one, they had to be about the South, and two, they had to be fiction.

So I read many novels, many short stories, plays—all written by white writers—because there was such a limited number of works at the time by black writers in a place like Vallejo. I found most of the work that I read untrue and unreal to my own experience, yet because I hungered for some kind of connection between myself and the South, I read them anyhow. But I did not care for the language of this writing. I found it too oratorical, and the dialects, especially that of blacks, quite untrue. (Twain and Faulkner can be put into or left out of this category, depending on your taste.) I did not care for the way black characters were drawn. (Twain and Faulkner can be accepted or not accepted here—again, depending on your taste.) Whenever a black person was mentioned in these novels, either she was a mammy, or he was a Tom; and if he was young, he was a potential Tom, a good nigger; or he was not a potential Tom, a bad nigger.

When a black woman character was young, she was either a potential mammy or a nigger wench. For most of these writers, choosing something between was unheard of.

Despite their descriptions of blacks, I often found something in their writing that I could appreciate. Sometimes they accurately captured sounds that I knew well: a dog barking in the heat of hunting, a train moving in the distance, a worker calling to another across the road or field. Pasternak once said that Southern writers wrote well about the earth and the sun. These writers, who so poorly described blacks, did well with the odor of grass and trees after a summer rain; they were especially adept at describing the sweat odor in the clothes of men coming in from the fields; you could see, better than if you were actually there, the red dust in Georgia or the black mud of Mississippi.

I read all the Southern writers I could find in the Vallejo library; then I began to read any writer who wrote about nature or about people who worked the land. So I discovered John Steinbeck and the Salinas Valley; and Willa Cather and her Nebraska—anyone who would say something about dirt and trees, clear streams, and open sky.

Eventually, I would discover the great European writers. My favorite at this time was the Frenchman Guy de Maupassant—de Maupassant because he wrote so beautifully about the young, and besides that he told good stories, used the simplest language, and most times made the stories quite short. So for a long time it was de Maupassant. Then I must have read somewhere that the Russian Anton Chekhov was as good as or better than de Maupassant, so I went to Chekhov. From Chekhov to Tolstoy, then to the rest of the Russians—among them Pushkin, Gogol, and Turgenev, especially Turgenev's *A Sportsman's Sketches* and his *Fathers and Sons*. The nineteenth-century Russian writers became my favorites, and to this day as a group of writers of any one country, they still are. I felt that they wrote truly about peasantry or, put another way, truer than any other group of writers of any other country. Their peasants were not caricatures or clowns. They did not make fun of them. They were people—they were good, they were bad. They could be as brutal as any man, they could be as kind. The American writers in general, the Southern writer in particular, never saw peasantry, especially black peasantry, in this way; blacks were either caricatures of human beings or they were problems. They needed to be saved or they were saviors. They were either children or they were seers. But they were very seldom what the average being was. There were exceptions, of course, but I'm talking about a total body of writers, the conscience of a people.

Though I found the nineteenth-century Russian writers superior for their interest in the peasants, they, too, could not give me the satisfaction that I was looking for. Their four- and five-syllable names were foreign to me. Their greetings were not the same as greetings were at home. Our religious worship was not the same; icons were foreign to me. I had eaten steamed cabbage, boiled cabbage, but not cabbage soup. I had drunk clabber, but never kvass. I had never slept on a stove, and I still don't know how anyone can. I knew the distance of a mile—never have I learned the distance of a verst. The Russian steppes sounded interesting, but they were not the swamps of Louisiana; Siberia could be as cruel, but it was not Angola State Prison. So even those who I thought were nearest to the way I felt still were not close enough.

I wanted to smell that Louisiana earth, feel that Louisiana sun, sit under the shade of one of those Louisiana oaks, search for pecans in that Louisiana grass in one of those Louisiana yards next to one of those Louisiana bayous, not far from a Louisiana river. I wanted to see on paper those Louisiana black children walking to school on cold days while yellow Louisiana buses passed them by. I wanted to see on paper those black parents going to work before the sun came up and coming back home to look after their children after the sun went down. I wanted to see on paper the true reason why those black fathers left home—not because they were trifling or shiftless, but because they were tired of putting up with certain conditions. I wanted to see on paper the small country churches (schools during the week), and I wanted to hear those simple religious songs, those simple prayers—that true devotion. (It was Faulkner, I think, who said that if God were to stay alive in the country, the blacks would have to keep Him so.) And I wanted to hear that Louisiana dialect—that combination of English, Creole, Cajun, black. For me there's no more beautiful sound anywhere—unless, of course, you take exceptional pride in "proper" French or "proper" English. I wanted to read about the true relationship between whites and blacks—about the people that I had known.

When I first started writing—it was about when I was sixteen or seventeen—my intentions were not to write polemics or anything controversial. At that time I had not read much writing by black writers, so I did not know what especially a black youth trying to write his first novel was supposed to write about. (I still don't know what a black writer is supposed to write about unless it is the same thing that a Frenchman writes about—and that is what he feels deeply enough inside of him to write about.) No, when I first started writing, I wanted to write a simple little novel about people at home. I think the first title I gave it was *A Little Stream*, because it dealt with two families, one very fair, one dark—separated from each other by a stream of water. But I gave the novel at least a dozen different titles before I was finished with it. Whenever the plot took a sudden change—a direction beyond my control—I erased the original title and gave the manuscript one that was more fitting.

The book I started in 1949 or 1950 was finally published in a completely different version in 1964 under the title *Catherine Carmier*. I had changed the title many times in those fifteen years. When it came time for publication the book was simply called *Catherine*. My editor wrote me a letter saying, "Listen, you ought to give it another title." I said, "*Catherine* sounds all right to me." Once

I had been in love with a girl named Catherine, and, too, I had just finished reading Hemingway's novel *A Farewell to Arms,* whose heroine's name is Catherine. I figured what was good enough for Hemingway was good enough for Ernie Gaines. So I said, "What's wrong with *Catherine?*" My editor said he thought something else ought to go with it. I said, "All right, her last name is Carmier, call her that. Call her anything—as long as I don't have to think up another title. Because then I'd have to write a new book—and I'm tired." So in 1964, it was called *Catherine Carmier.* It was published in Germany, and they called it *It Was the Nightingale.* And that came after they had even left out one of the main chapters in the book.

But let's go back to '49 ('49 or '50), when I first started writing. I wrote the manuscript out on sheets of paper about half the size of regular notebook paper. Where I got paper that size I've forgotten. Whether I typed the manuscript in single or double space I can't recall either. I do know that it was not typed well, because I had rented a typewriter for that single project without knowing where the letters A and B were located. I worked twelve hours a day at times, typing with two fingers until I got tired. Then I would lean on one hand and type with the index finger of the other. Finally, it was done—it had taken me all summer to do it. (I should mention here that before trying to type the novel, I had written the novel out in longhand. So it took me that entire summer to type it up and send it out.) After sending the manuscript to New York, I expected any day to receive a telegram telling me that I had written a masterpiece, and I thought a check of several thousand dollars would soon follow. But nothing of the sort happened. I supposed after the editors had shaken the little package, which was about half the size of what a manuscript ought to be, and found that it was not a bomb, and after they had smelled it and found that it was not a fruitcake, they quite possibly played football with it a few weeks when they had nothing else to do. Then they sent it back to me in the original brown paper, tied with its original broken and knotted strings. Only by now the paper and strings were a little dirtier than they were when I sent the manuscript out. I broke the strings and paper loose, found the blue or pink or yellow rejection slip, and took the rejection slip and manuscript out to the incinerator. Of course I felt the great letdown all beginning writers do. I had envisioned thousands of dollars, a nice place to live, a car, clothes of all kinds, and money to send back to my younger brothers, my sister, and my aunt. I was let down when it did not go that way. But between the time that I sent the manuscript out and the time it came back—a couple of months, at least—I had decided no matter what happened I would continue to write. So when the manuscript came back in its original wrapper, tied with its original string, yes, I felt let down, but I was determined to go on. I had only lost the first battle; I had not lost the war—yet.

From then on, school and working in summers kept me from writing another book, so I did not try again until I went into the army. I tried to write one in my off-duty hours, but I found that I liked shooting pool, playing pinochle, and playing softball too much to stick to the pencil. All I got accomplished was a short story that was good enough to take second place on the island of Guam, where I was stationed. The story was sent to our command headquarters in Japan to compete with all the other short stories by GIs in the Far East. There it got honorable mention. So I made fifteen dollars for second prize on Guam and ten dollars for honorable mention in Japan. I cashed the ten-dollar check as soon as I received it, but the fifteen-dollar check is at the house in a little glass bank that belonged to my aunt, who died in 1953. After her death, the bank was given to me to remember her by.

I was discharged from the army in 1955, and I enrolled at San Francisco State College. When I told my adviser that I wanted to be a writer, he asked me what else I wanted to be. I told him nothing else. He broke down the percentage of those who made their living writing. It was frightening. Then he told me the percentage of blacks who made their living writing. This was ten times as frightening. I told him I didn't care how hard it would be, I could not think of anything else I wanted to do. He saw that I was not going to change my mind, and he said, "You can't study writing here because you cannot get a degree in writing." (I should note here that you could take writing classes at San Francisco State at the time, but you could not major in writing. You can do either now.) He said, "You can't study writing here because you can't get a degree in writing. And in order to stay in college you must study toward a degree. So there." "All right," I said. "What is the closest thing to writing that I can study here?" "I would say English," he said. "When you fail at your writing, you can always teach English." "All right, I'll take that," I said.

For the next two years at San Francisco State and a year at Stanford, I tried to write about Louisiana. I wrote every free moment I had, and many times I disregarded my textbooks in order to write. There was something deep in me that I wanted to say—something that had been boiling in me ever since I left the South—and maybe even before then. My instructors at San Francisco State and Stanford thought I would say it all one day—but it would take time. "It will take time and work, time and work," they said. "Now you ought to read this," they said, "and read it carefully. Do you see how Turgenev handles this same kind of situation? Bazorov's relationship to his old people in *Fathers and Sons* is the same as what you're trying to do to Jackson and Aunt Charlotte. Now, take Joyce—see how he handles Stephen and his discussion with the priest. Sherwood Anderson—how he handles his people of Winesburg, Ohio. Faulkner—and his Yoknapatawpha County. Read, read, read it carefully. You'll get it. But it will take time—time and work. Much work."

In 1962, I realized that to write a novel about Louisiana, then I, too, should go back to the source that I was trying to write about. It was then that I decided to go to Baton Rouge to stay awhile and to work. I stayed six months, beginning in January 1963. I'd work five or six hours during the day, then take a nip or two at night—and I had much fun. I met some of the most wonderful people in the world. I talked to many people, but most of the time I tried listening—not only to what they had to say but also to the way they said it. I visited the plantation that I had tried to write about while I was in San Francisco. Many of the people whom I had left nearly fifteen years before were still on the plantation. Some were dead, but the ones living could talk about them and did talk about them as though they had simply walked into another room only a few minutes before. I stayed in Baton Rouge six months, and six months after I went back to San Francisco, I finished the novel that I had been so long trying to write. The novel was *Catherine Carmier*.

In the beginning the novel was twice as long as it was when it was finally published. I had put everything into those seven hundred pages that I could think of. I wanted everything that I had experienced, that I knew or had heard of about Louisiana. There were house fairs, with gumbos and fried fish, soft drinks and beer; there was much lovemaking, and, of course, there had to be illegitimate children; there were deaths, wakes, funerals, baptisms, even threats of race violence. But my editor thought I had a little too much and that the book ought to be cut in half. Stick to the simple love story between the boy from the North and the girl in the South and leave everything else out. After we had exchanged a few bitter words through letters and over the telephone, and after I had called him a few choice names that I think all writers call all editors, I finally took his advice. The book was then published, but just as soon forgotten.

Now where would I go from here?

Most of what was published in *Catherine Carmier* had taken place in the late fifties or early sixties. But what about my life before then? What about the people I really loved and knew? And what about the language—that language that is like no other?

It seemed that I could not think of another novel about Louisiana no matter how hard I tried, so I tried to write about San Francisco—the bohemian life in San Francisco, which I knew a little about. I wrote one novel in six months, another in about the same amount of time—and another novel about six months later. Within a year and a half or two years, I had written three of the worst novels that have ever been written by a published writer. I realized from those efforts that I was not a San Francisco writer—or at least not yet. And if I was not, then what—what then? Since I could not think of another Louisiana novel, what could I do? I got a job working with a printer. And when anyone asked me what I was doing, I told them I was learning the printing business. "What about your writing?" they asked me. "I don't know. Maybe I'll put it down," I said. But even when I was saying this, my mind was only on writing—writing something else about Louisiana. I knew that I had more to say—and eventually it would come—but when and how, I didn't know.

Then one day I was playing some of my records, and a particular verse caught my attention. I should note here that I'm an avid record collector. I have over five hundred LPs of all kinds of music—jazz, blues, spirituals, European and African folk music, American Indian music, etc., etc. I think I have learned as much about writing about my people by listening to blues and jazz and spirituals as I have learned by reading novels. The understatements in the tenor saxophone of Lester Young, the crying, haunting, forever searching sounds of John Coltrane, and the softness and violence of Count Basie's big band—all have fired my imagination as much as anything in literature. But the rural blues, maybe because of my background, is my choice in music. So, I was sitting around listening to a record by Lightnin' Hopkins, and these words stuck in my mind: "The worse thing this black man ever done—when he moved his wife and family to Mr. Tim Moore's farm. Mr. Tim Moore's man don't stand and grin; say 'If you stay out the graveyard, nigger, I'll keep you out the pen.'" These words haunted me for weeks, for months—without my knowing why, or what I would ever do with them.

Then I came back here in 1965, and a friend of mine and I were talking, and during our conversation he told me that someone we knew had been killed by a man in Baton Rouge, and that the person who had killed him was sent to prison for only a short time and then released. When I heard this, I had no idea that this incident could have any connection with Lightnin' Hopkins's blues verse. But the two things—the murder and the song—stayed in my mind, stayed in mind so much that I began to wonder what I could do with them. Then I recalled hearing about two other incidents in which blacks had murdered blacks. In Case One, when a white lawyer offered his services for a small fee, the prisoner told him that he would rather go to the pen and pay for his crime. But in Case Two, the prisoner left with his white employer. Remembering the first incident, I wrote the long story "Three Men," which was published in my *Bloodline* collection. But the second incident would require much more time and thinking. What would I do with my young killer once I got him out of prison? It took about a year, I suppose, before it all jelled in my mind, and then I started writing, in the summer of 1966, the novel *Of Love and Dust*. The novel takes place the summer I left the South. The action takes place on a plantation along False River. I used that particular place and that time because I knew more about them than I did about Baton Rouge. And I think I also used that time and place because, again, I was trying to say something about my past, something of what I had left out in *Catherine Carmier*. I wanted to talk about the fields a little bit more, about the plantation store, the river, the church, the house fairs, etc., etc., etc. And yet, when that novel, *Of Love and Dust*, was finished, I realized that I had done only a small part of what I had intended to write. I still had not gone far enough back. Jim, my narrator—who was a man thirty-three years old—though good, was not able to say all that I wanted him to say. Even when I brought Aunt Margaret, someone twice his age, to help him out, they, both together, could not say it all.

Before I wrote *Of Love and Dust*—sometime around 1963 or

1964—I wrote a short story titled "Just Like a Tree." The story was about an old woman who had to move from the South during the civil rights demonstrations. The story was told from multiple points of view—that is, several people telling a single story from different angles. Most of the people were her age, and while they were telling you the reason she had to leave, they were also telling you something about themselves. But they were only touching on their lives; they were not going into any great detail. In the case of Aunt Fe, the protagonist in the story, you only hear snatches of conversation about her life. You know that she must leave the South because they are bombing near her home and she could be killed. But you don't know her life—where she comes from, her children, her husband— her life, in general, before that particular day.

Now, I did not know when I wrote the short story "Just Like a Tree" in 1963 or 1964 that four years later I would start out from that idea and write a novel, *The Autobigraphy of Miss Jane Pittman*. As I've said before, at this time I still had not published *Catherine Carmier*; nor did I have any idea that I would write another novel, titled *Of Love and Dust*. But after these two books had been published, as well as the collection of stories *Bloodline*, I realized that I was writing in a definite pattern. One, I was writing about a definite area; and two, I was going farther and farther back into the past. I was trying to go back, back, back into our experiences in this country to find some kind of meaning to our present lives. No, Miss Jane is not the end of my traveling into the past—she is only another step back so that I can see some meaning in the present.

I knew at least two years before I started writing *The Autobiography of Miss Jane Pittman* that eventually I would write it. Maybe I had known it all my life, because it seems that I started writing it many, many years before, when I used to sit on the porch or the steps and write letters for the old people. But it took me at least two years after I first conceived the idea to start working on the book. I held back as long as I could because I knew I did not know enough. I had an idea of what I wanted to say—I wanted to continue from "Just Like a Tree"—where a group of people tell the life story of a single woman. But this woman in "Just Like a Tree" would live to be 100 years old—110, to be exact—with her life extending over the last half of the nineteenth century through the first half of the twentieth. But did I know enough to try such a project? The narrative technique would be easy—I had done it already in "Just Like a Tree"—but what in the world would these people talk about that could possibly fill five hundred pages?

After the *Bloodline* stories, I realized that in order to tell what I wanted to say about the people and the place, I had to go much farther back in time. *Catherine Carmier, Of Love and Dust,* and the *Bloodline* stories were easy writing, and I was writing about things that could have happened in the South during my lifetime, but I wanted to go farther back now, to a time before I, my parents, even my grandparents were born.

In the fall of 1967, I visited Alvin Aubert, a friend at Southern University in Baton Rouge. We sat in the living room while his wife prepared dinner in the kitchen. I said to him, "Al, what were those old people talking about when they visited my aunt and when they talked all day on the porch around the fireplace and at night? I can remember that they talked and talked, but I cannot remember what they talked about. You see, Al, I have this idea for a novel; it is about a 110-year-old woman who is born into slavery. I want the people to talk about her and in their rambling to reveal her story as well as their own. The story will happen between 1852 and 1962—from slavery to the civil rights demonstrations of the 1960s. What do you think they would have talked about?"

Where to start? With slavery, what the old people could have heard from their parents and great-grandparents about slavery. Next we discussed Reconstruction, the hard times. We discussed the Freedmen's Bureau. We discussed Lincoln, and Douglass, and Booker T. Washington because I could remember as a child a photo collage of the three hanging over the mantel in my aunt's room, just as I would see photo collages of John and Bobby Kennedy and Martin Luther King hanging on the walls of other African Americans in the 1970s. We talked about national heroes such as Jack Johnson, Joe Louis, and Jackie Robinson, about President Franklin D. Roosevelt, about the First and Second World Wars. After the national events we discussed state events—the great floods of 1912 and 1927, the cholera epidemic in New Orleans, the voodoo queen Marie Levaux, Huey P. Long and his men, the insane asylum in Jackson, the state penitentiary at Angola.

So we covered the nation and the state; next we came to the parish. We talked about the towns, the sheriff, the river, the people who lived along the river; we talked about the black professor who had been killed in 1903 for trying to teach young African Americans to read and write and to look after their health. His grave is on the bank of False River, about five miles from where I was born. My wife, Dianne, and I go by there all the time to stand in silence a moment.

After we discussed the parish we discussed the plantation and the quarter. We discussed the crops and the seasons and the work. We talked about the big house where my own grandmother worked for so many years; we talked about the store where the people bought their food and clothes. We talked about long days, dark nights, little pay, and mean overseers. We talked about hunting and fishing and gathering fruit that grew wild along the ditches and bayous. We talked about the church, about baptisms, about the cemetery, about unmarked graves. We talked about one-room schoolhouses and the teacher who came to the plantation to teach us children six months out of the year. We talked about a distant sound, the marching of the men and women for civil rights and their spokesman, a young Baptist minister from Georgia.

Al and I must have talked eight or nine hours that day and on into the night. After dinner when I got ready to leave, Al said to me,

"Now this is what they could have talked about; now you have to convince the readers that this is what they did talk about." I remembered that the old people spoke of seasons and not the name of the month. They spoke of cold, cold winters and hot, hot summers when it rained or did not rain, when the pecan and cane crops were plentiful and when they were not. When I asked them for the year, they would tell me, "Well, I ain't for sure." As a child I remember hearing them talk about the great flood and the boll weevils that came after the flood, but they could not remember the year. Yes, they knew the horror of the flood: they knew how swift the water moved one day, how slow the next. They could tell you the color of the water, they could describe the trash and the dead animals that the water brought, but they could not tell you what year except that it happened around the time that Huey Long was just beginning.

But I needed more; I needed dates, months, years. I needed to know whether it happened during the week or the weekend, whether it was spring, summer, fall, or winter. I had visited LSU in Baton Rouge several times to talk to professors in the English department and to give readings, but I had never been to the library. Louis Simpson at LSU recommended I go to the Louisiana room and speak to Mrs. Evangeline Lynch. When I gave Mrs. Lynch a list of all the information I needed, she said, "My God, are you sure?" I said, "Yes, ma'am." She had heard of me through the *Bloodline* stories, and she was happy to meet me, but she thought I was taking on a task much too big for me to handle. "Well, let's start looking around," she said; "we have a lot in here, my, my." When I received the Louisiana Library Association Award for *The Autobiography of Miss Jane Pittman* in 1972, Mrs. Evangeline Lynch was in the audience. She stood and waved as I told the people how she had helped me find information and how she had sent information to me in San Francisco, where I was writing the book. Twenty-two years later, when I received the same award for *A Lesson Before Dying*, she was again in the audience. She had long since retired and was a bit frail, but she stood up and waved as I told the people what she had done for me so many years before.

Mrs. Evangeline Lynch helped me get material from books, periodicals, magazines, newspapers, but I still had to go to the people. I still had to go out to the field. Mr. Walter Zeno liked his vodka and he liked his wine, and whenever I came back to Louisiana from San Francisco I would rent a car in Baton Rouge and go out to the old place with one of his favorite bottles. He would squat, not sit, on the porch by the door and drink and talk while I would lean back against a post, listening to him. He knew my grandparents' grandparents and all the others, white and black, who lived on that plantation the first eighty years of the twentieth century. Either by being directly involved or by getting this information vicariously, he knew everything that had happened in the parish during that same period. But he dated events by seasons, not by the calendar, and I had to go back to Mrs. Lynch or to one of the other libraries to find out exactly when it had happened.

Many of the local things could not be found in books or in newspapers. For instance, I have never found any written information about the professor who was killed in the parish in 1903; but when you asked about him, the braver ones—white or black—could tell you exactly how the weather was that day, and they could tell you it happened at the turn of the century, but they did not know the exact year. His tombstone, placed on the grave some seventy years after he was murdered, gave me that information.

I started writing *Miss Jane Pittman* with this idea of narration in mind: that different characters would tell the story of her life in their own way. The story was to begin on the day that she was buried— the old people who had followed her body to the cemetery would later gather on the porch of a lady who had never walked in her life, and there they would start talking. In the beginning there would be only three or four of them, but around midnight, when they were still talking, there would be a dozen or more. And by now they would be talking about almost anything—Miss Jane would be only part of their conversation.

I followed this multiple-point-of-view technique for a year—then I discarded it. (I should mention here—I should have mentioned earlier—that the original title was *A Short Biography of Miss Jane Pittman*, and that it was changed to *The Autobiography of Miss Jane Pittman* when I decided to tell the story from a single voice—Miss Jane's own.) I decided to change the way of telling the story because I had fallen in love with my little character, and I thought she could tell the story of her life much better than anyone else. The others were making her life too complicated in that they had too many opinions, bringing in too many anecdotes. I thought a single voice (Miss Jane's) would keep the story in a straight line. (Though, even here, I had trouble with her when she got wound up. Once the story really got moving, Miss Jane did and said pretty much whatever she wanted, and all I could do was act as her editor, never her adviser.)

Who is Miss Jane? What does she represent? I've heard all kinds of interpretations. More than one reviewer has said that she is a capsule history of black people of the rural South during the past hundred years. I must disagree, and I'm sure Miss Jane would, too. Miss Jane is Miss Jane. She is not my aunt, she is not any one person—she is Miss Jane. Maybe I had my aunt in mind when I was writing about her, but I had other old people in mind as well—those who sat on our gallery in the 1940s and those whom I've met on the road since then. You have seen Miss Jane, too. She is that old lady who lives up the block, who comes out every Sunday to go to church when the rheumatism does not keep her in. She is the old lady who calls a child to her door and asks him to go to the store for a can of coffee. She sits on a screened-in porch fanning herself in the summer, and in the winter she sits by the heater or the stove and thinks about the dead. Even without turning her head, she speaks to the child lying on the floor watching television, or to the young woman lying across a bed in another room. She knows much—she has lived long. Sometimes she's impatient, but most times she's just the opposite. If you take time to ask her a question you will find her to be quite dogmatic. You will say, "But that's not it, that's not it, that's not it." And she will stick to her beliefs. If you go to the history books, you will find that most of them would not agree with what she has told you. But if you read more closely you will also notice that these great minds don't even agree with one another.

Truth to Miss Jane is what she remembers. Truth to me is what people like Miss Jane remember. Of course, I go to the other sources, the newspapers, magazines, the books in libraries—but I also go back and listen to what Miss Jane and folks like her have to say.

This I try to do in all my writing.

I begin with an idea, this point, this fact: sometime in the past we were brought from Africa in chains, put in Louisiana to work the rice, cane, and cotton fields. Some kind of way we survived. God? Luck? Soul food? Threats of death? Superstition? I suppose all of these have played their part. If I asked a white historian what happened, he would not tell it the same way a black historian would. If I asked a black historian, he would not tell it the same way a black field-worker would. So I ask them all. And I try in some way to get the answer. But I'm afraid I have not gotten it yet. Maybe in the next book, or the one after, or the one after. Maybe.

Mozart and Leadbelly

In the early sixties, many of my colleagues were leaving the United States for Europe, Africa, Mexico, and so on, where they planned to write their great novels. They felt that America had become too money-crazed for them to live here and concentrate on their work. I was supposed to leave in the summer of 1962 with a man and his wife for Guadalajara, Mexico. I had been working on *Catherine Carmier* for three years but was getting nowhere with it. I had written it from an omniscient point of view, a first-person point of view, and a multiple point of view. I had changed the plot many times. Nothing seemed to work, and I figured it was because I needed to get away from the country, as my friends were doing. I was working at the post office during the summer of 1962 when my friend and his wife left for Mexico; I told them that I had to make some more money first, and that I would join them before the end of the year.

But something happened that summer of 1962 that would change my life forever. James Meredith enrolled at the University of Mississippi. Every night we watched the news—my family, my friends, and I—and it seemed that we cared for nothing else or spoke of nothing else but the bravery of this one young man. It seemed that when we spoke of his courage, I felt family and friends looking at me. Maybe it was just my sense of guilt. One night in October or November, I wrote my friends in Mexico a letter: "Dear Jim and Carol, I am sorry but I will not be joining you. I must go back home to write my book. My best wishes, Ernie."

I contacted an uncle and aunt in Baton Rouge, Louisiana, and they told me I could come and stay as long as I wanted to. So on January 3, 1963, a friend of mine drove me to the train station in Oakland, California, and fifty-two hours later I was in Baton Rouge. I had come back to Louisiana twice since leaving in 1948, but each time for only a week or two, and both times I lived with relatives out on the plantation where I was born. This time it would be for six months, and this time I would stay in town. I was determined to live as all the others did, and if that meant demonstrations and a run-in with the police, then let it be so. But at that time very few civil rights demonstrations were going on in Baton Rouge. And if the police did show up, they stood back watching but never tried to interfere physically with the gathering.

Uncle George and my Aunt Mamie had a four-bedroom house, and there were other people living in the house: their son, Joe, and three other nephews. Each Sunday we would drive out into the country to the old place where I was born and raised until I left for California. We would visit the old people, who would have dinner waiting for us—chicken, greens, rice, beans, a cake—and we would have lemonade and all sit down in the kitchen eating and talking. Then I would leave them and I would walk through the quarter back into the fields, and I would cross the rows where the cane had been cut looking for a stalk of cane that might have been left behind. On finding one I would peel it with my knife and chew it slowly, enjoying the sweetness of it. I would look back across the rows and remember when my mother and father and all the others in the quarter used to work these same fields.

And I would turn and look toward the quarter back at the cemetery where my folks had been buried for four generations, and I would go into the cemetery and look for pecans. If I found some I would crack them with my teeth as I had done as a small child and I would feel very comfortable and safe there because that is where Aunty, who had raised me, was buried. I did not know the exact place because the grave had never been marked, but I would feel more peace at that moment than I ever did in California.

By eight o'clock each weekday morning everyone except me would have left the house for work or school, and I would have the entire place to myself, along with my ballpoint pens, unlined yellow paper, and Royal portable typewriter. I would think about Catherine Carmier and Jackson and their families and loves and prejudices, and I would rewrite everything that I had written in San Francisco the past four years. I would work until about three or three-thirty and put everything away until the next day. Not long after arriving in Baton Rouge, I was introduced to a group of schoolteachers, and in the early evenings we would meet in restaurants, where we would sit and talk. When I was not with this group, I would go to a bar to join my uncle and his friends. My uncle worked as a janitor for one of the local oil companies near Baton Rouge. By my uncle's friends I mean the hard laborers—those who did the dirty work. I would join them in a bar, and we would have a setup, which was a pint of whiskey, a bowl of ice, a pitcher of water, and maybe a bottle of 7 UP or Coca-Cola, and each man fixed his own drink. Many times when I reached into the bowl to get ice, I noticed bits of sand and gravel in the bottom of the bowl. At first I was apprehensive; maybe I did not need ice after all. But after looking at these guys, who appeared pretty healthy to me, I concluded that a little dirt would not kill me either.

Baton Rouge was a dry town on Sundays; so I, along with some of the younger men, would go across the Mississippi River into Port Allen, down to the White Eagle bar. The White Eagle was a rough place, and there were always fights, but I wanted to experience it all. One novel, *Of Love and Dust*, and a short story, "Three Men," came out of my experience at the White Eagle bar. I knew now why I'd had such difficulty writing my novel in San Francisco: I had lost touch with this world that I wanted to write about. After living in Baton Rouge for six months, traveling across Louisiana, fishing in the river, hunting in the swamps, eating in small cafés, drinking in bars, writing five hours a day, five days a week, I was ready to go back to San Francisco to finish my novel. By then I had received an education in Louisiana history, geography, sociology, and its people that my books in California never could have given me and my running away to Mexico would not have helped. I started collecting blues records while attending San Francisco State College in the mid-fifties and inviting friends to my room to listen to the music. Most of the whites would listen to the records out of curiosity; this was before the Rolling Stones of England had made white America aware of the art and value of black blues singers. The white boys and girls of San Francisco wanted to listen because it was "exciting." However, very few of my African American friends from the college wanted to listen to it at all because they wanted to forget what those ignorant Negroes were singing about. They had come to California to forget about those days and those ways.

A lady friend of mine in Washington, D.C., once told me that she knew a young African American male who would always get in an elevator whistling a tune of Mozart. I, too, like Mozart; I like Haydn, Bach, Brahms, Schubert, Chopin. I like *Pictures at an Exhibition* by Mussorgsky, *A Lark Ascending* by Ralph Vaughan Williams—I like them all. And though Mozart and Haydn soothe my brain while I write, neither can tell me about the Great Flood of '27 as Bessie Smith or Big Bill Broonzy can. And neither can describe Louisiana State Prison at Angola as Leadbelly can. And neither can tell me what it means to be bonded out of jail and be put on a plantation to work out your time as Lightnin' Hopkins can. William Faulkner writes over one hundred pages describing the Great Flood of '27 in his story "Old Man." Bessie Smith gives us as true a picture in twelve lines. I am not putting Faulkner down; Faulkner is one of my favorite writers, and what Southern writer has not been influenced by him in the past fifty years? What I am saying to that young man who found it desirable to whistle Mozart in the elevator is that there is some value in whistling Bessie Smith or Leadbelly.

After publishing *Catherine Carmier*, my first novel, I tried publishing my *Bloodline* stories. *Bloodline* in the title means the common experience of all the male characters from the youngest to the oldest; they were all part of the same experience in the South at that time, between the 1940s and the 1960s. I thought that the stories were good enough and long enough to make a book. My editor, Bill Decker at Dial Press, felt the same way, but he told me that I needed another novel out there before he would publish the stories. *Catherine Carmier* had not sold more than fifteen hundred copies, which meant that hardly anyone had heard of the book. "Write a novel," the publisher told me, "and we will publish both the novel and the stories." "But those stories are good," I said; "they will make my name." "We know that," they said, "but no one knows your name now and we need a novel first."

On the plantation where I grew up in the forties were some tough people and mean people and hardworking people; they could load more cane, plow a better row, control their women—most of them would brag about having more than one woman. When the plantation system changed to sharecropping, many of these people left the plantation for the big cities, and there was always news about them getting into fights and getting themselves killed or sent to Angola State Prison for life. H (yes, that is a name) was one of those tough guys; he was tall, very handsome, and tough. He was shot point-blank when he was trying to climb through a window after hearing that his woman was with another man. Two or three months after this happened, I was back in Louisiana, and a group of us went over to the White Eagle bar. One of my friends pointed to a guy three tables away from us and said, "That is the fellow that killed H." "What the hell is he doing here?" I asked. "Shouldn't he be in jail?" "He was the good nigger," my friend said. "You don't have to go to the pen when a good nigger kills a bad nigger. A white man can pay your bond and you work for him for five to seven years."

I could not get that image of this guy sitting there in his blue silk shirt, blue slacks, and two-toned shoes from my mind, and back in San Francisco one day while listening to Lightnin' Hopkins and "Tim Moore's Farm," I thought about this guy at the White Eagle who had killed H. Suppose now, just suppose, I said to myself, you take a guy like this and you put him on a plantation to work off his time under a tough, brutal white overseer: what do you think would happen between the two of them? I wrote a first draft of this novel in three months and sent it to New York. My editor sent it back to me with this note: "I liked the first part of your manuscript; I liked the second part of your manuscript. However, the two parts have nothing in common but the characters. In the first half you have a tragedy; in the second, a farce. Go back and do it one way or the other; stick to tragedy." I wrote him back, "But the State of Louisiana did not see this as a tragedy. I have proof of that." Bill wrote back, "Too bad for the State of Louisiana."

And he was right about the novel. The first half was serious, the second was not. But I thought that if the State of Louisiana would not take the death of this young man seriously, why shouldn't I make a farce out of it? "Your Marcus killed another human being," Bill said; "you let him con the people on that plantation every way that he can, then you let him escape with the overseer's wife. No, that is not right; he should pay, or in this case let's take a different route." What happened in reality was that I rewrote the novel in three months and sent it back to Bill. He said that I had improved it 100 percent, but he told me to run it through the typewriter one more time, and he would publish both the novel and the *Bloodline* stories.

Bloodline is the beginning of going back into the past. I realized after writing *Catherine Carmier* that I had only touched on what I wanted to say about the old place and the people who lived there. My own folks are African, European, and Native American; they had lived in the same parish for four generations before me. My siblings and I are the fifth generation, and my brother's children are the sixth. There are no diaries, journals, letters, or any written words left by the old people, but there are people on that plantation who could tell me about my grandparents' grandparents and about the other old people of that time. Some of the stories were horrible, others were funny, but they were educational.

Until I was fifteen, I lived with my aunt, Miss Augusteen Jefferson. Because my aunt could not go to other people's houses, they would come to our house. They would talk and talk and talk, and I would listen. When there was no school and I was not needed in the fields, I often was kept at the house to make coffee or serve water. I also wrote letters for the old people. I have been asked many times about when I started writing, and for years I said I started at the age of sixteen. Now that I think back, I started writing on that plantation at the age of twelve. I had to be creative even then. Once the old people said, "Dear Sara, how are you? I am fine. Well, I hope you are the same," it would take them the rest of the afternoon to finish composing that letter. So I learned to write what I thought they would like to say and to write it fast, if I wanted to join my friends and play ball or shoot marbles.

Not very long ago in Mobile, Alabama, a reporter asked me about what I thought of the minority students who did not want to study dead white writers. I told him that I learned a lot from the works of dead white writers, especially dead white European writers such as Ivan Turgenev, Anton Chekhov, and James Joyce. These are the writers whose work I studied as a student at San Francisco State in the fifties because there were no books in the curriculum by black, Asian, or Hispanic writers. And I told him I could understand the anguish of these young people for wanting to read the work of their own people. I said what the curriculum should include is works by live and dead African American writers, live and dead Asian writers, and live and dead Hispanic and Native American writers, as well as live and dead white writers.

While I was a student at Stanford in the late fifties, my writing professor, Wallace Stegner, asked me, "Who do you write for? Who do you want to read your book?" "I do not write for any particular groups, Mr. Stegner," I said, "I have learned too much from other writers, American and European, writers who definitely were not writing for me or about me." "Maybe not for you, Ernie, but many had a particular reader in mind. Now let's say a gun was put to your head and that same question was asked, 'Who do you write for?'" "Well, in that case, Mr. Stegner, I would probably say that I write for the black youth of the South to let them know that their lives are worth writing about, and maybe in that way I could help them find themselves." "Suppose a gun was still at your head and you were asked for another particular group you wished to reach." "Well, in that case I would say that I also write for the white youth of the South to let them know that unless they know their neighbor of over three hundred years, they know only half of their own history."

A VERY BIG ORDER:
RECONSTRUCTING IDENTITY

A fifteen-year-old boy is standing on a riverbank in South Louisiana with a worn-out leather suitcase at his feet and a white pocket handkerchief in his hand. There is no way he can possibly imagine what he will be forty-one years and four months later, in December of 1989.

He is tall, thin; he is worried and frightened. But he continues to stand there as steadily as his legs will allow, because he knows he must go. He must go not only for himself, but for the others as well, because he will be the first male in the history of the family to go away and finish school. It had been planned by the others—if not planned, dreamed—long, long before he was aware of it and definitely long before he was aware of who he was.

There are others about him, his brothers and friends. They are not leaving home, so they are much more relaxed: they can play, chasing one another alongside the highway and up and down the riverbank.

Where the boy stands, he can see the road from which he has just left—the quarter. He cannot see his own home—it is too far down into the quarter—so he cannot see the old people who must still be sitting out on the porch with his aunt.

An hour ago he was packing his suitcase to leave. The few pieces of clothes—two shirts or so, but no more than three; two extra pairs of pants, underclothes, and an extra pair of shoes. Then there was the food that the old people had brought him, fried chicken, bread, tea cakes, pralines, probably oranges, and some unpeeled pecans. After he had finished packing, he tied up the suitcase and looked around the room. His ancestors, who had once been slaves, lived, if not in this house, then in one just like this one in the quarter. (He would be told that much later by a man who had spent all of his life here.)

The bus came around the bend of the road and he waved his handkerchief, and when the bus stopped he climbed on with the suitcase, and after paying his fare, he went all the way to the back of the bus where he was supposed to go, passing under the little signs hanging over the aisle that read "White" and "Colored." He must have found a seat because he cannot remember standing all the way to New Orleans, where he would take a train to California. But he can remember that until he got to Southern California he saw no other white person in his car except the conductor. When he changed trains in Los Angeles, he noticed the different races together.

His mother and stepfather now lived in government-subsidized projects in Vallejo, California. In the projects were blacks, whites, Asians, Latinos—all the groups, races, who were Californians at that time. He got along with the blacks immediately, but it took him a while to get up enough courage to approach the others. He watched them play basketball, football, tennis. He had never done any of this, so he watched them. Eventually he would be a member, but now he stood back and watched everything that was going on around him.

One day while he and one of the Asians stood on the sidelines watching a football game, the Asian said to him (and he still cannot recall what brought it about) that he, the Asian, was not as good as white people are, but better than blacks, because blacks had not contributed anything to civilization. They, he and the Asian, were watching a football game, and from what he could see of the game, the black kids were holding their place as well as or better than any of the other group. So what was this little fellow talking about?

He had never thought himself less than anyone else, nor better. He had come from a world where the two races, white and black, were separated, but he had never thought he was less than anyone else. He had always carried his share of the load. He had gone into the fields at eight years old, and he could do as much work as any other eight-year-old could do. He had gone into the swamps at eleven or twelve, and he could pull the saw as well as anyone of that age could. So he had never thought less of himself than he did of any other. There were those who were stronger than he, those who were better ballplayers and marble shooters than he, but he was better in other things than they were—reading, for example; writing letters, for example. So he had never thought himself less. So what was this little fellow talking about?

Once upon a time there was a tall, slim, frightened black boy who sat in the back row of all of his classes in California. Once he was called on to explain what he knew about the American Civil War. None of his teachers in the South had ever mentioned the Civil War to him that he could remember, and he thought his instructor had asked him what he knew about the silver war. He did not know anything about a silver war either, but he talked about a minute through the laughter of his classmates—until the instructor told him to sit back down.

This same boy was also told by other recent black migrants to California that you were never supposed to tell people you came from the country. Best to say you don't know a thing about picking cotton, or chitlins, beef tripe, watermelons—and all the rest of that country stuff like pig feet, pig lips, pig ears, pig tails. And you came from New Orleans—and never say N'awlens. It's New Or-lea-ans. Which he tried to do for several months—until someone asked him about Bourbon Street. He knew nothing about Bourbon Street, and he realized that to go on lying to others meant lying to himself. Not only was he lying to himself, but he was also denying knowing the others, the ones he had left, and wasn't that the same as denying who he was?

But it seems that we've skipped too far ahead. A while ago we were concerned with a young man who was searching for that elusive "I." Part of it he found by reading American, Russian, and French literature. Now he had to sit and think: how could he relate this to the lives of his ancestors and to the people whom he had grown up around; how to articulate their, his own people's, experience; how to articulate thoughts that they had been denied to articulate for over three hundred years? There were those recent migrants to the West who told him that digging into the past would be embarrassing, too painful; forget the past. But he wanted to become "I." And to do that meant to confront the past.

An interviewer from one of the more popular magazines would ask him one day, "What book of all those you read helped you to become the person you are today?" After thinking awhile, he shook his head; he didn't know. "Maybe it was the one that was not there," the interviewer said, "and you felt that you had to put it there."

His first effort as a writer was a love story between light-skinned and darker-skinned blacks, whose religions were Catholic and Protestant. He knew something about each because he had both in his own family. After five years of wrestling with the idea—articulating it was the problem for him, so as not to embarrass anyone—the book, or one little chapter, as he would call it, was finally accepted for publication. In the book he would have the main character say, "I feel like a dry leaf, broken away from the tree and now drifting with the least bit of wind toward no true destination."

In each of the following books he found that he was moving farther and farther back into the past until he realized that to find the tree from which the leaf had been broken was to go back to those who sat out on the porch the day he left. What were they talking about that day while he was inside packing? What did they talk about the day before, the year before, years and years and years before? Because his aunt was crippled and could not go to them, they came to her, summer and winter, day and night, weekdays as well as weekends, and talked. Sometimes in English, sometimes in Creole; sometimes their voices would hush when he came into the room. What was so secret, so painful that they did not want him to know? Why did they say it was none of his business when he asked the question?

His aunt as well as many of the others were dead by now—twenty years later. He went to the younger ones, their children, their nieces, nephews, and asked could they recall a phrase the old ones liked using or a song they liked singing. Was there a Bible they liked holding even though they did not know the words, or a hymnal they had saved even though they could not read a verse?

Recently, at a high school in Lafayette, the writer was asked by a white student what was an American. The writer told the student that he had been searching for that answer for nearly forty years now. The student asked, "Do you think you will ever find out?" The writer said he did not know, but he could not think of anything else more important in his life to do. The student said, "Well, I sure got a lot out of Miss Jane Pittman." The writer asked him what did he get. The student said, "Well, er, I, er, er—well, she made you think." Good, the writer said. That's good.

Bloodline in Ink

I left Louisiana for California in August 1948, not with a chip on my shoulder but with a block of oak wood in a sack on my back. I didn't know what it was, its meaning. I only knew it was there, and it was heavy.

I decided I would try my hand at writing. Writing a book shouldn't be too difficult; look how many books there were in the public library.

I began by writing longhand, just as I still do with the first draft. Then, in the summer of 1950, I convinced my mother to rent me a typewriter. I had gone through my book in longhand; now it was ready for typing. I knew absolutely zero about typing. Later, it would be proven that I knew even less about writing a book. Anyway, my mother rented the typewriter for me that summer of 1950, and for twelve hours a day I pecked and pecked with my right index finger. (I should mention here that my mother had had a baby in '49, and I had to babysit and write my novel all at the same time that summer of 1950.)

So I did everything to keep Michael asleep while I worked on my novel. I found that if I kept something over his eyes awhile—my fingers, preferably (I only used one hand while typing, so the other one was always free)—he would eventually go to sleep, giving me time for my work. Later that summer, I wrapped up my manuscript and sent it on to New York. My little package probably looked more like a bomb than like a novel to the New York people, because it was returned to me later. And I took it to the backyard and burned it in the incinerator.

I had read many books in the Vallejo library, but I had read only what I wanted to read, what I liked reading. Now I had to read what was needed to make me a writer, if I was to be a writer. Now I had to look deeper into the story or the novel, into what the writer was really trying to tell us; now I had to analyze form, which I had never thought of before. "Read Twain," they said, "especially *Huckleberry Finn*; read Faulkner as much as you can; read Hemingway—see how 'grace under pressure' applies to you, to your people, especially to your athletes. Read Eudora Welty and Steinbeck; read James and Conrad. Have you read Flaubert?"

"No, I've read de Maupassant."

"Read Flaubert. Have you read Cervantes and Shakespeare?"

"A little Shakespeare, but no Cervantes."

"Read *Don Quixote*, and as much Shakespeare as you can. And the Russians?"

"I've read Turgenev and Chekhov."

"You must read Tolstoy's *War and Peace*; Dostoyevsky's *Crime and Punishment*; Gogol's *Dead Souls,* and *The Inspector General* if you have the time. Read Thomas Mann. Read him. Read James Joyce's *Portrait of the Artist as Young Man*, and you should also read *Dubliners*. Forget *Ulysses* and *Finnegans Wake* for now. Read T. S. Eliot."

"I don't like that man. I don't understand anything he's talking about."

"Read him. When you begin losing your hair and your teeth begin loosening in the gum, you'll understand him. Read. Read.

Read. You want to say something about your people? You did say you wanted to say something about your people, didn't you?"

"Yes."

"Then read, read, read—the tools of the trade. There are other tools that you'll discover later, but these I recommend, and they are worthy tools, I assure you."

So I read and I wrote, read and wrote. In all classes except creative writing I made average grades. In creative writing, only As. So I knew I was determined to be a writer. Everything pointed that way.

After San Francisco State College, I went to Stanford for a year. On leaving Stanford, I went back to San Francisco, where I rented a one-room apartment with a Murphy bed. A Murphy bed is one that you push into the wall during the day and pull out at night. Besides the bed, there were a small couch and two chairs in the room. I had a small kitchen, a small bath, a small hallway with a small dining table. The dining table would be my desk. There I was determined to make my name. From that small table, I would write the books that would bring me the Pulitzer and the Nobel Prizes, and lots and lots of money—I thought.

Earlier, I mentioned leaving Louisiana with a block of wood in a sack across my shoulder. Now this block of wood must reappear in my narrative. Chekhov said so. According to Chekhov, if a gun is over the mantel when the curtain rises, then it must be taken down before the curtain's final descent. Therefore, being an admirer of Chekhov, I must include this block of wood somewhere in my story. Which reminds me of something else. One should never title a speech. Speeches should be either untitled as paintings are untitled or numbered as symphonies are numbered, but they should never be titled. Titles are so hard to stick by. (Many years ago I saw a French movie, one of those New Wave French movies of the fifties and sixties. It might have been *Rififi*—I'm not sure. But, anyway, the people inside the theater were advised not to reveal the ending to the people who were waiting in line to come inside. One fellow came out of the theater and told everybody in line to look out for the little white dog. Some people cursed him, some challenged to fight him, but he got away. We went into the theater and waited for the little white dog to show up on the screen. It never did.)

Anyway, earlier I mentioned a block of oak wood, and according to Mr. Chekhov, I must do something with that block of wood before closing.

But first, since the block of wood in the sack was only a symbol, what was its meaning? And again, as you may recall, I said that I didn't know its meaning. Only that it was there, and that it was heavy, a burden to carry.

Now let's go back to that one-room apartment with that block of oak wood in mind. In that room, I began to wonder what I should write about. At San Francisco State, at Stanford, on Guam, and in my home in Vallejo before going into the army, I had tried to write about the South, the old place, the old people, my brothers and sister, my friends, my church, and my little school. I remembered the letters I had written for the old people, the letters I had read for them. I thought about how I had gone to the store for them, how I had gone to the post office for them, how I had run from one house to another, borrowing a little sugar, salt, flour, or lard for them. I remembered how I had listened to them when they visited my aunt. I remembered how I had traveled with another aunt all over Pointe Coupee and West Baton Rouge Parishes, selling cosmetics. This aunt who sold cosmetics was Catholic and Creole, and I remembered how she and some of the other old Creoles talked about "them crazy 'mericans there on them plantation." The other aunt, the one who had raised me, was dead now (she died in '53, the same year I went into the army), but I could still remember her crawling over the floor, and cooking the food, and washing the clothes, and crawling across the porch to work in the vegetable garden beside the house after the sun had slipped behind our pecan tree. I could still see the rows of string beans and sweet peas and the rows of tomatoes and cucumbers where she worked.

In that small apartment sitting at that small wooden table, I could still remember the day I left Louisiana. And I could see those faces who didn't wish to look back at me, the same ones for whom I had written and read the letters. And when they did look at me, no more than a glance. I saw in their faces their lives, the lives of their people, my people, the past. I saw in those faces at that moment what they would never be able to put into words. Now it began to dawn on me: the meaning of those letters that I had written for them. How I had had to create the letters. They would say, "Dear Sarah, I'm well." Then they expected me to carry on from there. I had to tell Sarah all that they *wanted* to tell her but couldn't. ("That's why you go to school, ain't it?" they asked. "Now say something to fill in both sides of that paper.") And afterward, they would give me pralines, tea cakes, or a nickel.

In that room, I realized the meaning of that block of wood. These people had let me go to California, but I still had to write their letters. They made sure of that. Together, they cut a heavy block from one of our oldest live oaks, put it inside a strong croker sack, and said, "Here, and don't you dare turn loose of that sack. You do, we'll hear 'bout it, yeah."

At San Francisco State and at Stanford, I was issued the hammer, the chisel, a grinding stone, and a few sharp knives to do the work. I got a part-time job at the post office in the evening; the rest of the time I was at the task.

A woman I had met while I was at San Francisco State told me how lucky I was to have this huge block of granite (she didn't know it was oak) to work on, when many others who wanted to work had nothing at all to work on. I thought, "No kidding"—only I didn't say "kidding." I thought, "You don't know the half of it. It wasn't my choice; it was theirs." But I didn't say this to the woman, because she was a nice woman, and she and I would be very close friends for thirty-one years, until she died in 1987. She told me in 1956 that she would help me in every way she could, that she would like to see the work when it was done. She said that during the time I worked on the block she would help me buy and select clothes, she would cook and bring me food—but she wouldn't give me money for whiskey or for other women.

I didn't argue with the woman because she was very nice, and I accepted what she was kind enough to give me. And when I had chiseled off a chip from the block and carved it as well as I could, I would take it to her, and she would say yes, but not quite. And we would have small glasses of Stolichnaya vodka and orange juice, and we would sometimes go to a movie. She liked foreign films, so we would see one of the great Eisenstein films, or a Truffaut, or maybe one of Kurosawa's films. Other times, we would go to a symphony, and always to a bookstore. There were great bookstores in North Beach and on Haight Street and Polk Street. Most of the bookstores had prints of famous paintings, and while she looked at the prints of Monet or Degas or Dufy, I would look at Modigliani and Van Gogh. Modigliani for the nudes, and Van Gogh for his country people. I like *The Potato Eaters* and the worker's shoes and the people sowing wheat in the field. All this reminded me of home—Van Gogh did, not Modigliani.

And after leaving the bookstore or seeing a great film, I would go back home to work on the block. And I would go back to the woman to show her what I had done, and she would say yes, but not quite yet. And sometimes I would get angry with her, and I would ask her what the hell she knew about it. But after returning home, I would go to a pay phone and call her and apologize because I knew that she only wanted me to do it right. So I would go back and work again. I don't know the number of hours or days or weeks or even months that I would put into one carving—but I do know that the

Chinese grocer knew I had bought many cans of pork and beans, because one day when I came into his store he said, "Ah, the writer, pok-n-bens."

"Did I say I wanted pork and beans?" I asked him. "Can't you wait till I order?" He waited, eyeing me. Laughing inside, not out. "I want a can of Boston baked beans," I said.

"Same shelf," he said with a nod.

Then back to the block. Hours and days don't matter. Ultimately I would take the little figure to the woman in Pacific Heights, one of San Francisco's most exclusive sections, where we could look out of the window and see the bay and Angel Island and Alcatraz and part of the Golden Gate Bridge. The woman always had classical music on the big German radio, and she tried to show me the difference between Beethoven and Brahms. Beethoven's Seventh and Ninth were her favorite of Beethoven's symphonies; she liked Brahms's Second and Fourth better than the First and Third. She tried to teach me the difference between the music of Ravel and that of Debussy. And she told me never to say Debussy, but to say De-be-see. She tried to get me to say Bach the way she did, but I told her it sounded as if I were trying to get phlegm from the roof of my mouth. "Have it your way, E," she said. "Remain ignorant." One day when I came to her apartment with one of my little carvings, I heard on the radio what I thought was a great piece of music. I asked her what it was, and she told me it was Modest Mussorgsky's *Pictures at an Exhibition*. She told me that if I listened closely enough, I would hear that the music was constantly changing, which meant that the viewer had moved from one picture to another. And she told me that if I listened closely enough, I could hear that each change was definitely different. "Just as characters should be different in a book," she said. "If you like the record, I will get it for you."

"I like it," I said. "I like it very much." And since then, music has always been one of the tools.

One day the woman said, "The work is getting better. We'll send it to the people in the big city and see what they think of it." So we did. And we got a message with the little figure saying, "Yes, but . . ." And I told the woman I was very tired and I doubted that I could go on. She pushed: "Yes, you can go on; I'll be there to help you go on. You're blessed."

"I'm cursed, not blessed; I'm damned," I said.

"You should be honored that they chose you," she countered. "One day you'll be thankful that you went on." (At that time, I thought the woman was crazy, and I thought myself crazier, but still I went back.)

Some nights, I would go for long walks in the wind and fog, and I would say out loud, "Please relieve this load from my shoulder. I don't need the honors. Pass it on to someone else who deserves it more." And when it was not taken away, I thought more than once about Ambrose Bierce. Why not walk away, as he had done, and never be heard of again? Some of my friends were going to Africa, Mexico, Europe. But on their return, they seemed worse off than before they left. I began to wonder if I had the nerve for the big drop from our famous Golden Gate Bridge. My aunt, whom I loved more than anyone else in the world, was dead now, so what did I owe this world? I owed this world nothing.

But back in that room, I would see those faces again, on the porch and by the fire. And I would see my aunt crawling over the floor, and cooking the food and washing the clothes, and never ever complaining. And I would see the faces of many of my friends who never had my chance. And I would pick up the hammer and the chisel or one of the knives and go back to work.

Twenty-five years later, it is I who have begun to search faces for that one to whom I can pass the tools. I'm not through with the block yet, but at the same time, I'm looking. And if you as teachers should find him or her before I do, then you pass on the tools. In the long run, he or she will not regret the favor.

Aunty and the Black
Experience in Louisiana

━━━━━━━━

When people ask me who has been the greatest influence in my writing, I suppose they expect me to say another writer or a teacher. And I have learned much from teachers and writers and books. But the greatest influence on me as a writer and a man has been my aunt, Miss Augusteen Jefferson. Not for what she taught me with words— she did not give me advice (on leaving her), as Polonius gave Laertes; but she showed me, without the use of her legs, that I could do almost anything with those twenty-six letters if I would only work hard enough at it.

Of course, I have not. I have not read half as much as I should have. And surely I don't spend nearly as much time at the desk as I should. Five days a week, five hours a day are too much for me. With her it was seven days a week, all day—and as far as I know she never had one day's vacation in her life.

You know, there's never a lack of others telling you what to do with your life. My young friends did not want me to write about the rural South, but about New Orleans—which I knew absolutely nothing at all about. Years later, when I was about to be discharged from the army, friends told me not to leave, because civilian life was pretty hard. In the army there was security. Jokingly they would add, "You will always have three beds here—one in the barracks, one in the hospital, and one in the stockade." There was no lack of beds, or food, and of course the whole army would be behind you. What more security does one need? So why leave? You're a bright young man, get along well with others, a born leader, can go to officers' school if you wish. What more should you want?

After leaving the army, I enrolled at San Francisco State to study English literature and creative writing. I was so far behind in general education courses that I could not take creative writing classes until the second semester. During my first semester I had to take expository writing 110—I shall never forget it, nor will I ever forget the teacher, Mr. Stanley Paul Andersen, who taught the class. On my first paper he gave me a D, the second a D+, the third a D–. Each time he gave me a D, he called me to his office; each time he called me to his office, I told him I would do better next time. When he called me the third time, I told him to let me try writing a short story, not a composition, which I found so restricted. He told me that this was a composition writing class, not a creative writing class, but if I thought I could explain things better in fiction than I was doing in composition, then go on and do it.

I wrote a story I called "The Turtles." Mr. Andersen liked it and passed it around to the other teachers, and later it would be the first story published in the new San Francisco State literary magazine. Miss Dorothea Oppenheimer, who was just starting her literary agency in San Francisco, saw the story and liked it, and she was my agent until she died. And I have been most grateful to Mr. Andersen ever since 1956.

You know, a teacher can only help just so much in preparing you for life—whether she is that crippled black woman on a Louisiana sugarcane plantation or a white professor of English in a western university. They can only open the door, and you must walk that old road alone. Often you fail the first time, but sometimes with that first failure, it makes you try just a little harder the next time. I don't know what would have happened to me had Mr. Andersen insisted that I write the composition. Had he slammed that door in my face rather than crack it open so I might walk through, I have no idea how long it would have taken me to open that door again. Still I have not done all the work I should have done. Not read the books, not spent the hours at the desk I should have.

Students are always asking me if I would add anything to the books I have published. I tell them yes, if I could write the books all over again. But those books are already out there, they're in the past, and I can't go back to them. I must put what I left out of them in the next book. But isn't this our main excuse? We're always saying that if we could, we would do it better, but of course we know we can't go back and redo, or do more.

I'm sure every student has heard his or her parents say, "If I had to do it all over again, I would . . . But . . . you must do it instead." We're lazy, we're not courageous enough, we all can do a little bit more, and we should. But we never do.

You know, when you get to a certain age, you stop doing and you start giving advice. Those who don't or can't do it, teach it. I find myself telling my students what the great American novel ought to be about. That decade between '58 and '68, King's Birmingham boycott to his death in '68. During that decade more people of all social, educational, and economic backgrounds—from the lowest peasant position in Mississippi, Georgia, Alabama, Louisiana, to the highest position in Washington, the presidency—were involved in changing social conditions in this country. Only because of those changes am I able to stand in the lists of American writers.

But there are still changes to be made, things to be done. We want you to do it, you, the bright ones out there. I tell my students that the great American novel using that decade between '58 and '68, if used well, can have the scope of Tolstoy's *War and Peace*. They ask me why not do it myself? I tell them I'm too lazy. It will require too much work, too much research. Haven't you heard that excuse before from the older ones? "I would do it . . . but . . ."

I remember back in the sixties when all the violence was going on in the Southern states . . . when I heard about it I would sit at my desk till I had written a perfect page. I would show the Bull Connors and the Faubuses, and the Wallaces and the Thurmonds that I could do anything with those twenty-six letters given to them by their ancestors—not mine—but do more with those letters to help not only my race, but also my country, than they could ever do to destroy it.

Many things have changed since then, since Wallace stood in the door of the school, since Bull Connor used his electric cattle prods, hosepipes, and dogs against American black men, women, and children. But there's still so much more to do.

Jonestown, Guyana. We should be howling still about what happened there. And I should be your leader. For surely it will happen again. Faulkner once said that the thing that will destroy us is our lack of fear. We must be afraid that things like the Guyana suicides can and will happen again, but we're not afraid. If it happened tomorrow and less than nine hundred people died, it would not make the front page for more than a day. We believe in records. If a 747 jet fell tomorrow and fewer than three hundred people died, it would make the front page only one day. Because, you see, more than three hundred people have died in the crash of a 747 jet before, and two hundred would not be significant enough. Two days, three days later, the story, if it is followed up at all, would end up on page five or six, and maybe continued on page ten.

Back to Guyana . . . I knew many of the people who died there. I knew the beautiful blond young lady from Arizona who was in charge of the old people in San Francisco. For a while they lived in the same apartment house I did. The young lady and I used to talk all the time. When they went to Guyana, the barracks where the old people were quartered was called "Miss Jane Pittman's Garden."

And that Sunday when I heard what had happened, I was angry, but I did not howl loud enough. I did not howl loud enough or long enough. And because I did not howl as loud as I could, and because I continue to watch certain religious leaders on television, I am certain Guyana will happen all over again. Only it will not be in Guyana, but here. Maybe not with cyanide in Kool-Aid. Maybe it will not affect the physical body at all. But it will be the same. Simply because we do not howl.

You don't have to be a writer to howl. You can be a student of math, engineering, any of the sciences, law, agronomy, architecture—this world is yours, and it is you who must keep it sane, or surely Guyana will happen again. Next time it may not be nine hundred, but nine million, or ninety million, or nine hundred million. We must howl against the insanity going on around us day after day after day.

We must howl at some of the interpretations of the Constitution. The Constitution is a good piece of work, one of the greatest pieces of work done by man; but there are men who interpret, bend the Constitution for their own selfish needs, interpret it in ways so that certain Americans are not ever likely to appreciate all that America has to offer.

There were men on television who would swear that the Bible tells us that a country like Russia would one day influence a country like Cuba to go out and spread its Communist, anti-Christ views over Africa as well as the Americas. You must reread the Bible. And if it is not there, say it is not there. Because if you don't, Guyana can happen again—will happen again.

Black students are always asking me, "Why do so many of your young men of vision die in your novels? You seem to kill off the braver ones. Are you trying to discourage us from trying?" I tell them that my young men die because they're not *supposed* to have vision. They're *supposed* to accept the status quo. They're *supposed* to accept that what is will always be, or wait till others change it for them, but not they themselves. The young men in my novels and short stories who die cannot wait until others change the condition, because the condition then may not ever be changed.

I tell the black students who ask me why must my young men die that young men who tried to change conditions have always died. Two thousand years ago a child was born who would be nailed to a tree thirty-three years later for trying to change conditions. Today, so much of what that young man died for has been interpreted so poorly that other young men may have to die in order to get it back in the right direction.

We live in a world of myths. We live by myths daily. You must destroy the old myths, create new ones. John Wayne was a myth. There were only a few cowboys like John Wayne. Most of your cowboys were small men, very, very poor. There were many blacks and Mexicans among the cowboys. It was a tough job, a dirty job, and you did that only when you could not get anything better. It was not nearly as romantic as John Wayne and John Ford would make it seem.

Myths can be changed—but only you can change them. Children can be fed all over the world, and should be fed, but only you can feed the children. Wars must be stopped, but only you can stop wars. Men must live and work together, but only you can make this happen.

Your parents, your ancestors have done so much, yet there's still so much more to be done. We lead the world in technology—students from the rest of the world come to the United States to be educated—we send a man to the moon, and bring him back safely; we take the heart out of a dead man and put it into another man so that he may live a few years longer. Yet we cannot live side by side, or worship in the same church. Eleven o'clock on Sunday is still the most segregated hour in the United States.

Someone told my generation to make these changes and someone told the generations before mine to do it, and the generation before that. Two thousand years ago a child was born, and he was asked to do it because the others had failed. The Son asked, "Will you be there with me? I am of the flesh, I'm weak." The Father answered the Son by saying, "Yes, I will be with you." "Then I will go," the Son said. "I will do my best." "That is all I ask of you," He said to the Son.

WRITING *A Lesson Before Dying*

I was teaching at the University of Louisiana at Lafayette when I came up with the idea for *A Lesson Before Dying*. And that would be around 1983 or 1984. Now, the original idea was that the story would occur in the early 1980s. I wrote a letter to the warden at Angola, the state prison here in Louisiana, and informed him who I was—that I was a teacher here at UL, and that I was the author of *The Autobiography of Miss Jane Pittman* and several other books, and that I had another novel in mind about a prisoner on death row, and would he, the warden, mind if I asked him a few questions. Question number one: Would it be possible for someone not kin to the condemned man who was not a minister of religion or his legal adviser to visit him on death row? About a week later, I received a letter from the warden's office informing me that the warden would not be able to guarantee me that kind of security. I immediately wrote a second letter, assuring the warden that I, Ernest J. Gaines, had no intention of visiting Angola on a regular basis, but that I was writing a novel (and I emphasized the word *novel*), and I was wondering if it was possible that such a person—a teacher, for example—could visit a condemned man. Well, the warden's office never did answer my second letter, and maybe that was a blessing in disguise.

Being a writer-in-residence on any university campus, you're constantly being asked how's the writing coming along, and when can we expect the next book, etc., etc., etc. *A Gathering of Old Men* had been published in 1983, so between '83 and '85 I was between books. That is, I was not writing. When a colleague of mine asked me what I was doing, I told him I had a novel in mind and that I had written the warden at Angola. I told him the results of my second letter. I gave him the general plot of the novel, of a young man being in the wrong place at the wrong time, and he was charged with murder. Paul Nolan, my colleague, told me that he knew of a case I might be interested in reading about. The case Paul was referring to concerned a young man, a seventeen-year-old boy, who had been sentenced to be electrocuted in the electric chair here in Louisiana. Something happened that day with the chair. It did not work properly, and the boy was *not* executed, but put back into his cell to await what next step the governor would take. Paul told me he realized that the two cases didn't sound the same—sound alike—but I might benefit by reading his case and that he had a lot of material about the case if I would like to do so.

This particular case he spoke of having happened about '46 or '47 appeared familiar to me, and around a time I had written about in previous stories—"The Sky Is Gray," "Three Men"—and the novel *Of Love and Dust*. Besides that, the case Paul Nolan referred to happened only a few miles from where I was now teaching and no more than seventy miles from where I had lived as a child and the area where most of my previous stories had taken place. There were so many similarities—the work, religion, the food that people ate, everything. The case Paul recommended could have happened in the parish where I grew up. The stories are different, still I would use some of the information from the previous case. Both young men are black. Both nearly illiterate. Both were involved in the murder of a white man. In Paul's case, the young man confessed to the murder. My young man would maintain his innocence to the end. No defense witnesses were called in either case. Only white men served on the juries. This was the forties, so there were no women and, of course, no blacks on the juries. After reading all the material that Paul had given me, I asked myself, "Why not bring my story back to the forties?" If I put the story in the forties, there was so much material I could use. I could use the plantation as home for my characters. I knew life on the plantation because I had written about it in several other books—*The Autobiography of Miss Jane Pittman, Of Love and Dust,* and the stories in *Bloodline.* I could use the church school for background, the church where generations of my folks had worshipped and where I had attended school my first six years. I could use the crop as background—when it was planted, when it was harvested. I knew the food the people ate, knew the kind of clothes they wore, knew the kind of songs they sang in the fields and in the church.

So the best thing to do was to bring my story back to the forties, the period I knew and where I was most comfortable. I read everything Paul Nolan gave me to read and all he recommended. His young man would lose and be executed a year and a week from the day when he was first placed in that chair. The case went all the way to the Supreme Court in Washington, where it lost by a decision of 5 to 4.

Because I teach creative writing at the university and because I teach at night, I have a chance to draw people from outside the university, and I always get attorneys. I've had one or more in each class since I started teaching in the university in 1981. All have a dream of being a Scott Turow or a John Grisham. One of my students had a condemned man on death row. And I would always ask him questions about his client, especially what emotions did he show knowing that he was going to die on a certain date, at a certain hour. I could always tell when my student had visited with his client because of the tired and painful look he brought into the classroom. He was much older than this young man, and through the years he had gotten very close to him. He had gotten too emotionally involved, and he knew it, and it showed.

He, the student of mine, helped me in many ways. He brought me pictures of the state prison, pictures of the electric chair—"Gruesome Gerty." I asked him more questions. I asked him what kind of wood was the chair made of, how much does the chair weigh, how wide and thick were the straps that went around the arms and legs of the condemned. And I kept a picture of the chair on my desk, especially while writing the last chapters of the novel.

Another colleague of mine knew someone whose father-in-law was the sheriff of a small town. She asked me if I would like to meet the sheriff. I think he was an ex-sheriff by then, but everyone still called him sheriff. When we arrived at the house, I was introduced to the sheriff, to his wife, and to another man. The sheriff's wife served us coffee. I was served last, and I saw how much her hands shook when she served me. I was certain that she had never served coffee to a black man before, but after all, I had written *The Autobiography of Miss Jane Pittman* and also knew someone who knew her daughter-in-law. So she, of course, could show some of her Southern hospitality. The sheriff and the other man wanted to know where I came from, did I like the South, how long had I been teaching at the university. I told them I was born and raised about sixty miles from where we now sat, that my people had been there since the time of slavery, and that I had been teaching at the university for about five years, and I liked it very much. That relaxed them a bit, and we finished our coffee. I asked the sheriff the same question I had proposed to the warden in my letter: "Could someone who was not a close relation, a minister of religion, or a legal adviser visit someone on death row?" The sheriff told me that in the case of a parish jail it would be entirely up to the discretion of the sheriff. He told me that the sheriff of the jail was totally in charge and that he made all the decisions. Now, that bit of information was extremely vital. I had to find a reason to pressure the sheriff into allowing someone whom he may not even like into visiting the prisoner.

Some of my colleagues at the university would ask me how the novel was coming along. When I would tell them that I was still try-ing to get everything straight in my mind, some of them would offer advice. One fellow who considered himself a writer, too, said find something on the sheriff that he would not want people to know about. I told him it sounded like blackmail, and I didn't want to have anything to do with that. He told me he had another idea— the sheriff's wife had had an abortion in the past, and you know how these Southerners felt about that. I told him I didn't care for that idea either. He said, Well, let's say the sheriff's wife had had a rela-tionship with a black man and your character threatens to expose it. By God, that would light his fire—"and more than likely get my character killed before he ever got to the jail. No thanks," I said.

The original idea of the novel, when I thought the story would take place in the eighties, was that Grant, the narrator, would have been living in California, and he would come to Louisiana one sum-mer to visit his aunt and eventually get involved in visiting the young man on death row. That was the original reason for the ques-tions about whether someone other than a legal adviser or a minister could visit him, because I'm sure the sheriff would not want an out-sider, especially someone from the North, interfering with his busi-ness. It was not until I decided that the story would take place in the forties that I would make Grant a teacher who had gone away for his education and then returned to teach on the same plantation where he was born and raised and where all of his people had lived for sev-eral generations. However, because he was educated, the sheriff still may not have wanted him to be there.

My colleague at the university had given me an idea about how to solve my problem when he mentioned the sheriff's wife several times. I would not cause her to have an abortion or a black lover, but I would put her in a position where she would pressure her husband into allowing Grant to visit Jefferson in prison.

On the plantation where I was born, my maternal grandmother worked at the big house as cook for many years, and I myself had worked in the yard there on several occasions, collecting eggs from where chickens had laid in the grass, gathering pecans, and picking fruit from the different trees. Now, suppose I made the sheriff's wife a member of the family where my grandmother had worked all these years. Wouldn't she, my grandmother, have done favors, extra favors, for members of that family? Would that be enough reason for her to feel that she could go to them for a favor, which I thought would be a better reason—and more convincing to the reader—to get the sheriff to allow the narrator to visit the prisoner? So I created two elderly women. They were Tante Lou, the narrator's aunt, and Miss Emma, the prisoner's godmother. And those two would apply the pressure.

I have said that I wanted the story to take place in the eighties and that the narrator, Grant, would come from California. Once I decided that the story would take place in the forties, and that Grant had lived on the plantation all his life, had gone away to be educated, and had returned to teach, all this adds another element to the story. I didn't want just another story of someone waiting to be executed; that had been done many times before. To make my story different I had to do something else, and make Grant also a prisoner of his environment. Grant teaches in a church. As I said, I went to a church school the first six years of my education. Grant hates teaching. He hates the South. He hates everything around him. This is the forties, remember, and the professions for blacks to enter were extremely limited. You could be a teacher and teach black children. You could be an undertaker, a barber, an insurance collector from other blacks. You could own a small grocery store or a nightclub. But you could *not* be an attorney or a doctor. You could not be a banker or a politician and certainly you could not run for political office. Not in a small place like this in the South at that time. Grant wishes to run away. He's been well educated and he knows there's a better world somewhere else. But he has an aunt, Tante Lou, and just as she and Miss Emma exert pressure on the sheriff, they do the same to him to keep him in the South. Eventually he would become involved in Jefferson's plight, and in the end it would benefit both of them. He would teach Jefferson to live for a while and to die with dignity. Jefferson in turn would help him find himself.

In 1986, a young female attorney in my class asked me if I would like to meet the lawyer who had defended the young man whom Paul Nolan had spoken about. I told her I certainly would. She brought the old man to my house—a Cajun fellow, probably in his seventies, bent, frail. My student and I made coffee, and she had brought cookies, and we sat on the porch. It was this man who told me about the traveling electric chair. I had heard about it, read about it, but I had not spoken to anybody who knew about it first-hand. He told me about the generator that accompanied the chair because sometimes our Louisiana weather causes the electricity to be erratic. To avoid that problem, the state prison sent its own generator. We don't have the electric chair in Louisiana now, but some type of lethal injection is instead used for execution.

But let's go back to the late forties, when it did travel from one parish to the other. At that time the execution was administered in the parish where the crime was committed, not necessarily at the state prison, as it is today. This attorney told me about how the chair with the generator was delivered in a truck, a special truck that delivered it the morning of or the night before the execution. He told me that the time of day for execution in that particular parish was between noon and 3:00 p.m. on Friday. He told me the generator had to be tested before the hour of execution to be sure it was working in time. He told me you could hear the generator at least two city blocks away from the jail. He had witnessed the execution of the young man who had been sent to the chair a year earlier. During that year, this attorney had argued the case before the Appellate Court of Louisiana, the Supreme Court in Louisiana, and the Supreme Court in Washington. His argument was that it would be cruel and unusual punishment to send this young man back to that chair. But he failed in each court, and a year and a week from that first date, the young man was executed. Suddenly the attorney became silent and brought his hands up to his face. My student moved closer to him and held him. He laid his head on her shoulder and wept. Forty years later, he could still remember that generator, that chair.

Students are always asking me, "Do you know the ending of your novel when you start writing?" And I have always used the analogy of getting on a train from San Francisco to go to New York. It takes three or four days to get there. I know some facts. I'm leaving San Francisco for New York. I also know the states I'll travel through and some of the things I'll do. I know that I'll go to the dining car to eat. I'll go to the club car for a drink. I'll read the book I brought with me. I'll get so many hours of sleep. These things I know. What I don't know is how the weather will be the entire trip. I don't know who will get on the train and how they'll be dressed or where they'll sit. I don't know all the valleys and hills that I'll cross during my trip. I don't know all the different colors of nature, the colors of the leaves on the trees, the color of the different crops in the different fields. I don't know all the turnings and twists of the rail or when the train will make a sudden stop. In other words, I can't anticipate everything that will happen on the trip, and sometimes I don't even get to New York, but end up in Philadelphia.

When I started *A Lesson Before Dying*, I knew that Jefferson would be sentenced to die. Because in Louisiana in the forties, if he had been caught on the premises where a white man had been killed with a bottle of liquor in his hand and money in his pocket, that added up to guilt. But would he be executed? I didn't know for certain. Maybe the governor at the last moment would pardon him when the state could not definitely prove his guilt. The story could have ended there, because by now Grant could have reached him, convinced him that he was not the animal he had been so described in court, but that he was as much human as any of them and probably even more so. Because the story is not whether Jefferson is innocent or guilty but how he feels about himself at the end. However, the Cajun attorney gave me a different alternative. After he described that tarpaulin-covered truck delivering that chair and that generator on an early foggy morning, I knew that I had no other ending but that Jefferson would be executed. I wanted the reader to see that truck and that chair and to hear that generator.

Two things I had not anticipated when I began the novel and that would be vital in the story are the radio and the notebook. After I had gone so far into the novel and Jefferson still refused to communicate with anyone, I knew I had to find some way to make him talk. On that plantation where I lived as a child, on Saturday night the people of one or two of the homes in the quarter would give a house party—or a "supper," as we also called them. At these suppers, there would be food and drinks and music, the music coming from an old gramophone. On one of his visits to the jail, Grant mentions the music to Jefferson. When Jefferson shows some sign of interest, Grant promises to get him a radio so he can have some music to listen to. The idea of the radio was not planned, but it turned out to be a most important turn in the story. From that moment on, there was some communication, although limited, between the two of them. Still, Jefferson refuses to open up completely to Grant or his godmother, Miss Emma, or the minister of the church. So we know little of what he's thinking about or what he thinks about life. And I felt we had to know him better. Once I decided he would be executed, I knew, since he would not reveal his thoughts to someone, still in some way he had to give the reader some information. I didn't want any last efforts, speaking on the walk to the chair. I needed the information long before then.

Thus, the notebook. Grant would bring him a notebook and a pencil and tell him to write down anything he wished. His least little thoughts. When Grant visits again, he sees that Jefferson has written in the notebook and erased. And Grant tells him not to erase, never to erase, just go on and write his first thoughts the best way he can, which he does from then on. Jefferson is barely literate. He has never written a letter in his life. He was barely able to write his elementary school assignments. But now, with his pencil and notebook, he tries to define his humanity—in the few days he has left to live. He does not know whether to write above the lines or across the lines, so he does both. He does not erase. He does not capitalize. He uses no punctuation marks. He writes what comes into his mind. He writes at night when he has light because he does not want others to see him doing so during the day. He writes the night before his execution because the sheriff promises him that he can have all the light he wants on his last night. His diary is made up of small things, about the people he knew and how they affected his life, about insignificant incidents. He thinks about justice and injustice. And he wonders about God. All of this is written above and across the lines of his notebook, without capitalization and punctuation.

Grant does not attend the execution. Though he has worked hard with Jefferson, he does not have the courage to be there at his death. The young deputy brings Jefferson's notebook to him and tells him that Jefferson was the strongest man in that room when he came to die. The young deputy gives Grant this information outside the schoolhouse. When Grant returns to his class, his students are waiting, standing at attention, their shoulders back, heads high, to hear of the execution. Grant, cynical to this moment, looks at them, crying.

Writing for me is discovery. If I knew everything when I began a novel, I'm afraid it would be boring to write. I do not know everything that's going to happen in the book. I don't want to know everything. I want to discover, as you, the reader, want to discover, what it's all about. Those little unknown things that happen on the train between San Francisco and New York keep me writing and you, the reader, turning the pages.

Oprah Winfrey asked what I try to reach for in my writing. And I said something to this effect: I try to create characters with character to help develop my own character and maybe the character of the reader who might read me.

Stories

CHRIST WALKED DOWN MARKET STREET

I have been asked many times when will I write a story or a novel about California after having lived there forty-four years, and I always answer that I will, but only after I have written Louisiana out of my life—which I hope shall never happen.

That does not mean that I have not *tried* to write about California—and I emphasize the word *tried*. I have parts of short stories, parts of novels; first drafts of each, in boxes at Dupré Library. Once I tried a romantic novel based on *Othello*—love and jealousy—but no murder. After a first draft I put it away, because it did not sound right. (Shakespeare had done it so much better 360 years earlier.) I tried writing a novel about bohemian life in San Francisco, but after drinking a bottle of liebfraumilch wine along with a loaf of French bread with salami and cheese, mayonnaise and mustard, I became so ill that I realized the bohemian life was not for me. There was a period when I read nothing but ghost stories, and I thought I could write one, too. I have said facetiously that it was so real that I scared myself, but the truth is that it never got off the ground. (I lost interest in it, because at about that same time I came up with the idea of a life story of a little lady who would live 110 years.)

But whenever I had a manuscript or a novel in New York with my agent or my editor, I would, to pass away the time, resort to the short story. Sometimes the story would be about Louisiana, other times about San Francisco. The Louisiana story was always completed, the San Francisco story hardly ever. None was ever published.

Many years ago, the late fifties or early sixties, I read a story by Isaac Bashevis Singer titled "The Spinoza of Market Street." I have forgotten what the story is about, but I could never forget the title. Possibly because one of the main streets in San Francisco is called Market, and I have walked that street hundreds of times to clothing stores, movie theaters, record shops, and bookstores. And ever since I read that story by Singer, I've always wanted to write a story about San Francisco's Market Street.

While on a one-semester leave from the University of Louisiana at Lafayette in 1984, I taught creative writing that fall at the University of Houston-Downtown. The hotel where I lived overlooked one of the main streets, and many times I stood at the window, looking down at the traffic below. One day I saw a man shuffling along the sidewalk, holding up his trousers with his left hand, while he stuck out his right hand to others and begged for money. I had seen people beg on Market Street in San Francisco many times, but the image of this person stayed in my mind because I saw him probably once or twice a week. Always coming from the same direction, and he seemed to always wear the same clothes, trousers much too big and much too long.

After I had seen him several times, I thought I could write a story about him. Who was he? Where was he coming from? Where was he going? Did he have a home? Did he have a family? Was he alone? Now, not only did I have to create a story around this figure, but I also would have to find a title for the story.

For some reason, and I still don't know exactly why, the title of Isaac Singer's story came into my mind. It was a title that I could not forget any more than I could that person who shuffled along the sidewalk below the window of my hotel several times a week. Since I didn't know Houston well enough to write about it, I had to place the story somewhere else. Not in a small Southern town—my Bayonne, say—but in a large city: San Francisco. Use the rhythm in Singer's title, but place it in San Francisco. Singer: "The Spinoza of Market Street." Mine: "Christ Walked Down Market Street."

I must admit that I've rewritten this story at least a half dozen times since 1984 and am still not satisfied with it. Maybe I'll have to get the Louisiana stuff out of me first before I can write the story the way it should be.

But I've been asked for a story about California. So here goes.

You remember how it used to be when a bum was a bum, just a bum? No flower child, no hippie, Beatle, punker—nothing but a plain bum—you remember? You would have to go back twenty-five, thirty years—the late fifties, the early sixties, say. Back before Jack Kennedy was assassinated there in Dallas. Before Alioto had all these high-rises built here in San Francisco. About the time the Giants came to the city and had to play at the old Seals Stadium at Sixteenth and Bryant. Godamighty, I wish they were still playing at Seals Stadium and not in the goddamn icebox they call Candlestick Park. It makes me shiver just to think of that place. . . .

Well, now, thank you for the drink, sir, thank you for the drink. May all your days be sunny and bright, and your nights spent in the arms of some luscious babe. Only the best for a gentleman, sir, and I can tell by your attire that you are a true gentleman.

Sir, please do not take me for a drunk or a cynic. Maybe in some ways I am both—but I have not always been this way. As you see me, sir, in the past I have been as sober and sensitive, as compassionate, as loving, as giving and caring as the next man. Yes, sir, in the past I have possessed all these noble qualities. Yes, sir, I have. Yes, sir, I have.

Sir, I know the streets of San Francisco like very few men do. I am seventy-one now, and I have lived here most of my life. Oh, I have traveled this country many, many times—a job here, a job there—looking for something I know not what—but I've always returned to the city of St. Francis. Whored this town, drank this town from bar to bar, and walked this town from one end to the other. I've seen it all in this town, sir. Yes, sir, you're looking at a man who has seen it all.

To your health, sir. To your health. Yes, sir, I can see you're a true gentleman. Thanks for the drink.

Now, you take bums, sir. To be a true bum, it takes real talent, a genius. He knows man better than the psychologist. More clever than the novelist, or your poet. Knows more of man than your social scientist will ever know. (Shakespeare was right. Make your fool wise. . . . Oh, what Mr. William knew.) I respect the bum for that innate knowledge of man. Yes, sir, I do . . .

Sir, are you one of the chosen? Ah, I see by your expression you don't know what I mean by one of the chosen. Then I'll explain. The chosen is the one that the bum uses . . .

Let me explain, let me explain. Because if you're not a chosen, then you think bums bum off everyone alike. Well, you're right in a way, but only half right. The bum will alike beg off man, woman, or child, but unless you're one of the chosen he'll go so far and give up. But now with the chosen, he never gives up. He will hound and hound the chosen long as he can find him. He feels that the chosen owes him, and for some reason deep inside himself the chosen feels the same way.

Now, I know I'm getting a little philosophical. But that is true, sir, as night follows day and—et al., et al., et al. There are people—chosens; a word I thought of some thirty years ago—whom the bum will haunt when all others turn him down. For example, sir, you are looking at a 100 percent genuine chosen right now in the person of me. I am more of a chosen than your average chosen is. By that I mean I hunt for bums to give handouts; they don't have to hunt for me. Or I should say I did it in the past. . . .

Bend an ear, sir; bend an ear—as that master of English drama, Mr. William, would say. I shall say one more thing about the habits of bums, then I shall get down to the nitty-gritty, as the saying goes today. But again to your health, sir. Sunny days; nights of wine and love.

Take a bum now, sir. A bum can spot one of the chosen in a crowd of a thousand people. I've been at football games among eighty thousand people; baseball games where there were fifty thousand or more; crowded airports, bus stations, crowded streets. On the other hand, I've been on empty buses, just me and the driver. Driver picks up the bum at a bus stop—and guess what the bum does? Go on and guess; go ahead and guess. Give up? Then I'll tell you. He comes and plops down right beside me. Fifty, sixty empty seats—does he sit in one of them? No siree, bob. Plops down right beside me with his hand out.

Another example. Two o'clock in the morning. Twenty, twenty-five people on the bus. Hispanics, Asians, blacks, whites—name the races here in San Francisco, and they're on that bus. Bus stops, bum gets on. Passes the Mexican, passes the Chinaman, the black, Italian, the Russian; everybody; then plops next to me, his hand out already.

Take a good look at me, sir. Am I so different from other men—even, say, yourself? Maybe I need a shave; can stand a shower; a change of clothes I can use; a haircut, too, I suppose. But these are minor things. The major thing, do I look different from other men? And the answer is no. No. Still I am. Because I'm one of the chosen.

Now, to get to my story, sir. And it is a very short story. . . . But first, well, before I get started, the old throat gets a little dry after so much talking. . . . Well, now, thank you, sir. Thank you. And may all your days be sunny and—well, you know all the rest. . . .

I am a walker, sir. Walked most of the major seaport cities of this country. Longshoreman being my work, I've been to Seattle, Port-land, New Orleans, Boston, New York. You name them, and I've walked them all. But my favorite has always been and will be the city of St. Francis, San Francisco.

To walk around Stow Lake in Golden Gate Park at seven o'clock on a cool, windy morning, with that fog rolling in from the ocean, to smell the eucalyptus and the pine, not even your best wine is more intoxicant. Take Kennedy Drive to the Great Highway, stroll along Ocean Beach from the Cliff House to the zoo and back—that is a blessing for any man who loves land, wind, and sea. There are so many wonderful places to walk here in this great city, should I stand here all day I could not name half of them.

But bend an ear, sir, as Mr. William would say. My story does not take place in the park or on the beach. Neither does it take place in one of the more romantic settings in the city—the Mission, China-town, Fisherman's Wharf, Twin Peaks—no, sir. Market Street. Of all places—Market Street. Between Fifth and Sixth on Market Street.

It is raining, it's windy and cold. Twelve-thirty, maybe one o'clock in the afternoon. Umbrellas all over the place, but doing little good against the wind. Must be fifty, sixty people on the block, all in a hurry to get out of the weather. Myself, I had been to the post office at Seventh and Mission to cash a money order, and now I was on my way down to Roos Atkins to get a jacket that they had on sale.

I saw him maybe a hundred feet away. But I'm sure he had seen me long before then. There were probably a dozen people between us, so he didn't have too much trouble picking me out. And you have never seen a more pathetic figure in your life. Barefoot. Half of his denim shirt inside his black trousers, the other half hanging out. No belt, no zipper—holding up his trousers with one hand. They were much too big for him, much too long, and even holding them up as high as he could, and as tight as he could, they still dragged in mud on the sidewalk. From the moment I saw him, I told myself that I was not going to give him a single dime. I had already given a quarter to one who stood out in the rain in front of the post office.

As we came closer, I saw him passing the other people like they weren't even there. And they were doing the same to him, avoiding him like they didn't even see him. I could see from twenty-five, thirty feet away that he was angling straight toward me. I moved far to the right of the sidewalk as if I might go into one of the stores, but he knew I wasn't, and he moved over, too, and kept coming toward me. Then at a distance of about six feet away he reached out his hand in slow motion. The palm of his hand was black with grime, his fingers were long and skeletal, I went by him without looking into his face. I made two more steps, then I jerked around. Because I had seen something in the palm of that hand that looked like an ugly sunken scar.

But as God be my witness He was not there. He was not there, sir, He was not there. No one was within ten or fifteen feet of where He should have been. No, sir, I had not made more than two or three steps before I turned around. And I should have seen Him as clearly as I'm seeing you now—but He was not there. Just this empty space between me and all the other people. Just empty space.

I stood there searching for Him. I looked all the way to the end of the block. I looked across the street. He could not have entered one of the stores that quickly. But nothing, nothing. Only the people rushing toward me or rushing by. I couldn't possibly tell anyone what I had seen. They would have thought certainly I was mad.

I was terrified. And with all the traffic noise around me, I could still hear my heart beating—beating too fast, too loud. I forgot about the jacket, I went back home. I sat in my kitchen drinking a brandy, trying to calm myself. But I couldn't rest, and I came back to Market Street. It was raining harder, it was colder, but I had to come back. I walked that one block between Fifth and Sixth a half dozen times.

Late that afternoon, never mentioning it to anybody, I went back home.

I was a longshoreman then, working off Pier 50 in China Basin. Each evening when I got off I'd walk down Market Street. On days when I didn't get work, I would walk down Market Street. I wouldn't dare tell anyone what I had seen, afraid they would think I was crazy. But if I saw Him again I would tell the world and I wouldn't care what they thought.

Market Street became a second home to me. For a couple of years, day or night, I would walk down Market Street. When I didn't see Him again I got the idea that maybe He would not come back in that same form. Maybe He had already returned in a different form and I hadn't recognized Him. Maybe He was one of my neighbors.

Though I continued to look for Him as I had seen Him that first time, now I searched the face of anyone and everyone I passed. I also looked closely at the palm of all hands I came in contact with, whether it was the hand of one of the dock workers, black or white; whether it was the left or right hand of a store clerk, a bus driver when I got my transfer, or the butcher when he gave me my change—I looked at all their hands.

And I have searched thousands of faces. I have been insulted, threatened with violence for looking too closely in the face of man, woman, or child. You have no idea, sir, what names you're called for looking people in the face. And for Christ's sake, don't speak to a stranger. You speak to a strange woman, you're a possible rapist; to a man, you're labeled as a faggot; to a child, you're suspected of molestation. You're not supposed to speak to your fellow man anymore. Not anymore. At least a half dozen times the past thirty years I've been arrested for soliciting. And do you know what that means, sir, soliciting? It means looking closely into someone's eyes, hoping that He's Christ. Soliciting.

The people down at the Hall of Justice got so used to seeing me that they would hurry up and process me and kick me out on the street again as if I were some kind of San Francisco nut. Not nutty enough for the loony ward or even a halfway house—but just a benign nut, as though I were a certain kind of San Francisco character. So with a word of warning to not do it anymore—that is, look people in the face or speak to them—they would boot me back out on the street. And soon as they did, I would walk up Sixth to Market Street and begin all over again to search faces and hands, hoping that one of them would be His.

I began to think He might return in the form of the Trinity—Father, Son, and Holy Ghost. So I started concentrating on threes. Whenever I saw three men walking together I paid them very close attention. They could be white, black, Asian, or a mixture of the three. There could be three Jews or three Muslims, I would look them over. He's in all of us, so He didn't have to come back as any one race. I got so hung up on threes. One day I followed three Filipinos up Kearney Street. You see, by now I was looking for Him everywhere—not only on Market Street alone—but anyplace I happened to be. Of course, these little fellows I was following were much smaller than the figure I had seen that day on Market Street—but who is to say in what form He'll come back? Anyway, I caught up with them—and was sorry that I did. Two wore sports jackets and the third one wore a seersucker suit and a bow tie, and he had the greatest command of the filthiest language you have ever heard. He called me every kind of faggot he could think of. He even said some things about my mother no man should say to another man no matter how he looks at him. I tried to explain to him why I had followed them and why I had looked closely at them, but he told me that all us Frisco faggots were alike—only our approach was different. Again I apologized to him and his friends, and I was lucky to get out of there with my balls, because those little fellows can sure use knives.

I was in Golden Gate Park one day, walking down Kennedy Drive, near the flower conservatory. Twelve Japanese were outside, taking pictures of flowers. Now, there could have been more than twelve—maybe fifteen; and there could have been less than twelve—nine or ten. But to me they seemed like twelve, and since that was the number of His disciples I thought maybe He could be among them. I came up to them and started looking into faces. Not satisfied, I asked them to let me see the palms of their hands. They were very cooperative; you know the Japanese—all manners—bowing, smiling, showing me their hands. I had gotten to number eight when I was suddenly grabbed from behind and thrown into a police van. The people at the Hall of Justice remembered me, and didn't keep me in jail. They just told me to stay out of Golden Gate Park. I told them that I would—but I could no more stay away from that park than a priest from his church. I've walked in that park at least twice a week since the thirties. Especially on Sunday morning. That is my church. I'm closer to God there than any church building I've ever been in. When it's cold I wear my old army field jacket, and I put peanuts in the right pocket for the squirrels, and bread in the left pocket to feed the ducks and the geese. And I spend an hour out there with them, every Sunday. And I feel so close to God there, with the squirrels and the ducks and geese, and the eucalyptus and pines swaying in the wind, and the fog coming in from the ocean and floating over the lake like smoke—that is my church.

Not to say that I didn't go to any other churches, I went to many of them in search of Him. To the black churches in the Fillmore, to the upper crust in Pacific Heights, to churches in the Mission. For thirty years I've searched for that figure I'd seen that day. I've been arrested, beaten, robbed, knives held to my throat—all because I've looked too closely in faces and hands.

Sometimes on Sunday, when I came from the park, I would turn on my little black-and-white television set and watch the church services. I would watch any denomination and everyone I could find. But not once. Not once have I seen Him in the audience. Some of these hippies around here dress up like Him every now and then—but you can tell a phony when you see one.

Well, sir, that is my story. What do you think of it? Do you think it's fair to show up once and never again? Tell me what you think of that.

"You down there," I heard the bartender saying.

"You speaking to me?"

"Finish that drink and get out of here."

"I beg your pardon."

"I said finish that drink and get out of here," the bartender said. "You've been playing with that one drink long enough. You'll give the place a bad name."

"My friend bought this drink for me, and I'll take as long as I want to finish it."

"You've never had a friend in your life," the bartender said. "Finish that drink and get out of here."

"I do have a friend," I told him. "The gentleman who was in here a moment ago."

"What gentleman?" the bartender said. "You've been playing around with that one drink the past hour."

"You're crazy," I said.

"What did you say, you bum?" the bartender said, coming toward me.

"There was a gentleman standing right here talking to me," I said. "He wore a pinstripe suit and a trench coat. And he wore a felt hat, to the side. He had on a striped shirt and a red tie. He bought me three drinks, and you served it out of that bottle there."

The bartender glared at the bottle on the shelf. He started to look back at me, then he jerked his head around to look at the bottle again, staring at it for several seconds.

"Finish that damned drink and get out of here," he said to me. "Ain't nobody been in here but you."

"You're crazy or you're—"

"I'm what, you lousy bum?"

"Nothing. Nothing. But tell me once more. Tell me true. You honestly didn't see Him?"

"You've been the only one standing there the past hour," the bartender said. "I just bet you have a friend with a pinstriped suit."

"Why did you look at that bottle so long?" I asked him. "I'll tell you why. You got three less drinks in that bottle now."

"I can't remember the amount of liquor in every bottle in this bar," the bartender said. "Now, finish that drink and get out of here, or I'll throw you out."

"Just one more time," I said to him. "Please. One more time, you didn't see Him?"

"You've been the only person standing there the past hour," the bartender said. "Your clothes probably scared all my other customers away."

"Then I shall finish my drink and leave, sir. But before I go, let me tell you something, you're one of the most unluckiest men in the world. You don't have to worry about being a chosen one."

"Just get out of here," the bartender said.

"I'm on my way, sir. If I hurry, maybe I'll see Him again!"

The Turtles

When we got to Mr. James's house, my old man leaned the fishing poles against the fence and we went into the yard. Mr. James and Benny were sitting on the porch. Mr. James was fanning his face with his straw hat.

"It's coming down," my old man said. He put his foot on the step and leaned upon one knee. "You and Benny about ready?"

"Aren't you and Max going to rest awhile?" Mr. James asked.

"Better not stop too long," my old man said. "You don't feel like starting again."'

"I see what you mean," Mr. James said. "Get the poles, Benny."

"You want me to wake up Ma and tell her we're going?" Benny asked.

"She knows we're going," Mr. James said.

Benny went inside and got his hat, then he got the fishing poles from beside the house. He got the can of worms from under the steps where he kept them cool and moist, and we started out for Gillman's Lake. Gillman's Lake was about two miles from Mr. James's house, and we made it over there way inside of an hour.

It was quiet and cool around the lake, and the lake was as smooth and shiny as a clean mirror. Looked like you could lie on top of it, or walk on it, and not go under and get wet. There wasn't a bubble or a ripple on it, and a few leaves from the trees slept on top of it like cocoons on a twig. I felt like diving in with all my clothes on and swimming from one side to the other.

"Find yourself a can and bring me half of the worms, Max," my old man said.

I found a can down at the water where somebody had left it, and put about half of the worms in it. I gave my old man the other half, then I got my line. Benny and Mr. James divided their bait, then Benny and I moved down the lake to find a good spot to fish. We moved about a hundred yards from where my old man and Mr. James were, to a dead tree that had fallen out on the lake. We walked out on the tree—that is, I walked out on the tree. Benny crawled out on it, like he was afraid he might fall and get his clothes wet. I was hoping my foot might slip so I could fall in.

Benny and I sat sideways on the tree, and I could see my old man and Mr. James sitting down on the bank farther up the lake. They were talking and looking out at the lake.

"There's no fishes out here," Benny said.

"Give them time," I said.

Benny had a big stopper on his line because he didn't know how to fish too good, and the stopper lay on top of the water, leaning a little to the back, like it was waiting for something to grab the hook and pull on the line so it could dip right under.

"We're going to the baseball game next Sunday," I told Benny.

Benny didn't say anything.

"Why don't you ask Mr. James?"

"Ma'll never let me go," Benny said.

"Church, huh?"

"That's every Sunday," Benny said.

"Why don't you ask Mr. James?"

Benny looked at his old man down the lake.

"Shucks," Benny said.

Then something struck Benny's line, and Benny jerked the line up in the air.

"You can't catch anything like that," I said.

"Something was on it," Benny said.

"He was just playing around with the bait," I said. "You didn't give him enough time."

Benny drew in the line and looked at the hook. He covered the hook well with the bait, then he dropped the line into the water again.

"You have to let them run with it awhile," I told Benny. Benny nodded his head, and about a minute later, something struck his line again. The stopper dipped under the water a little, then it was still. It set still for a moment, then it began to move a little.

"Let him play with it for a while," I whispered.

Benny held the pole with both hands.

"Must be a little one," he said.

"Not too much noise," I told Benny.

The stopper went all the way under, and whatever was on the hook started to move toward the tree.

"Better pull it up," I said.

Benny jerked the line up out of the water, and a little turtle was hanging on the end of the line. Benny dropped the line back into the water.

"Pull him up," I said. "He'll tangle your line on the tree."

"I don't like to catch these things on my line," Benny said.

"Pull it up," I told Benny.

Benny pulled the turtle up out of the water again and tried to shake him off the line.

"He's swallowed the hook," I said. "You can't shake him off."

"You want to take him off for me?" Benny asked me.

"Benny, you're not afraid of a little turtle, are you?"

"I just don't like to mess with them," Benny said.

I looked at the little turtle hanging on the end of Benny's line.

"Here," I said, handing Benny my line. "Hold mine. I'll get him off."

I took the line on the bank and took the turtle off and killed it. I brought the line back to Benny.

"Did I have a bite?" I said.

"A little one," Benny said. "But he left."

"Did you pull up the line?"

"No," Benny said.

I drew in the line and saw that something had cleaned the hook. I baited the hook again, and threw it out toward the other side of the tree.

"I just don't like to mess with turtles," Benny said.

I didn't answer Benny, and we didn't talk anymore. We sat there about fifteen minutes, then Benny caught another turtle. I took that one off the line and killed it, then we moved from the tree. We found another spot farther down the lake, but we didn't have any luck there either. Even the turtles weren't biting there.

"They just aren't biting today," Benny said.

"I guess not," I said.

We moved down about fifty yards and threw our lines out into the lake, then we sat down on the bank. We figured that nothing was going to bite, and we made ourselves comfortable. Soon we were lying down on our backs and looking up at the trees overhead.

"Hey there," Mr. James said, standing over us. "You boys come out here to fish or sleep?"

We sat up and I pulled in my line. Nothing was on it, and the hook was clean.

"Where's mine?" Benny said.

"Something must've taken it," Mr. James said. "Why didn't you stick the pole in the ground like Max did?"

"I stuck it," Benny said.

"Well, no use crying over spilled milk," Mr. James said. "Come on, let's go."

"Must've been another turtle," Benny said.

"You all caught many?" I asked Mr. James.

"About a dozen, each," Mr. James said. "Maybe more. Your pa caught a nice trout farther up the lake."

I wound up my line and threw the rest of the worms out into the lake. Benny did the same thing with his cup of worms.

When we got down where my old man was, he was standing beside a tree with the pole in one hand and the fishes in the other. He had about twelve or fifteen perches on one string, and the trout on a stick. The trout looked like it was about two feet long.

My old man looked at me and Benny, then he started up the bank.

"Want me to carry the trout, Pa?" I asked my old man.

"You don't like to carry fishes," my old man said, without looking around.

I knew my old man was mad because I had gone to sleep and not caught anything. I wanted to say I was sorry, but my old man didn't like for me to say I was sorry about anything. So I dropped back and walked along with Benny.

"Here," my old man said. "Take it."

I ran up beside him and took the trout, then I dropped back and walked alongside Benny. Benny didn't like the way I was grinning and feeling proud.

My old man and Mr. James walked in front of me and Benny when we were going back home, and nobody was doing much talking. When we got to Mrs. Diana Brown's place, the sun was still about two hours up in the sky.

"We might as well stop in and have a drink of water," my old man said. "I'm a bit thirsty. Aren't you, George?"

"I can stand a drink," Mr. James said.

"Me and Max'll stay out here," Benny said. "I'm not thirsty."

"Come on in," Mr. James said.

"I'm not thirsty," Benny said.

"Come on in, anyhow," Mr. James said. "Might as well be sociable."

We leaned our fishing poles against the picket fence and went into the yard. Benny walked in back of us.

Mrs. Diana Brown was a widow who lived back in the fields with her grown-up niece, Amy. There wasn't another house within two miles of Mrs. Diana Brown's place, and none of the other women folks associated too much with her or Amy. They said that no woman with a grown-up niece like that was worth anything, if neither one of them was married. But that never bothered Mrs. Diana Brown.

She came out to the store every Saturday and made grocery and came back to her place without saying anything to anybody. Mrs. Diana Brown walked more prouder than any other lady that I had ever seen.

Amy was sitting on the porch when we went into the yard.

"Diana home, Amy?" my old man asked.

"She went to town," Amy said.

My old man looked at Amy.

"Well, we just want a drink of water," my old man said.

Amy smiled.

"Well's in the back," she said. "Help yourself."

My old man and Mr. James went around the house, and Benny and I stood out in the yard next to the porch. Amy looked at us, then she went inside the house. My old man and Mr. James came from in back of the house and sat on the end of the porch.

"It's been hot today," my old man said.

"Yes," Mr. James said.

Then they didn't say anything else and my old man took out his pocket handkerchief and wiped his face and neck. They didn't look like they were going to be moving soon, so I leaned against the steps to rest a while. Benny moved over to the big mulberry tree that Mrs. Diana Brown had in her front yard.

"Max," my old man said, "I want you to go into the house, and go into the first room on your right. Just push the door open and go in there."

"What for?" I asked.

"Because I said so," my old man said.

"Yes, sir."

I went up on the porch and into the house. I pushed the door open like my old man had told me to do, and I saw Amy lying in the bed under the spread. She was covered up all the way up to her neck.

"Hi, Max," she said.

I looked at Amy but I didn't say anything. The window right in back of the bed was opened, but the two curtains were very still. It had been a hot day and no wind was blowing. I looked at Amy grinning at me, then I backed out of the room and went back on the porch.

"Pa—" I started to say.

My old man jumped like something unexpectedly had hit him.

"What are you doing out here, Max?" he said.

"Amy is in there."

"I know she's in there," my old man said.

"She's in the bed," I said.

"I knew that, too," my old man said. "Go back in there like I told you."

I went back to the door, and thought maybe my old man had made a mistake about the room. I went back out on the porch.

"Pa, is that the right room?" I said.

My old man looked at me like he knew I was going to come back out there.

"Max," he said, looking at me, "if you come back out here one more time without going into that room and staying in there awhile, I'm going to take my belt off to you."

"Yes, sir."

I went back to the room where Amy was and stood just inside of the door.

"Max is afraid of girls," Amy sang. "You're afraid of me, Max?"

"I'm not afraid of anybody," I said.

"Then come here," Amy said.

"I rather stand here where I'm at," I said.

"Your pa want you to come where I'm at," she said, grinning.

I looked at Amy, and I wanted to leave the room again, but I thought about my old man. Not that he would whip me, I knew he had been bluffing out on the porch. He had never whipped me, and I doubted if he ever would. But that wasn't what I thought about. I thought about our friendship and our partnership. I had been his partner since Mom had died, and that had been a long time. And nothing had broken it up because I had always obeyed him. And I knew as long as I obeyed him the partnership would last. When I didn't, it would end. I wasn't ready for that to happen. So I went where she was like he wanted me to do.

When I went back on the porch, my old man was sitting with his back against the post. He had one leg drawn up on the porch. He gave me a glance as I passed by him, going to the end of the porch to sit down, but he didn't tell me anything. I looked at Benny sitting down on the ground against the tree. He had a little stick in his hand and he was poking in the ground. Mr. James was sitting next to my old man, looking down at his feet.

"Benny," Mr. James said.

And just like that, Benny started crying.

"Cut that out," Mr. James said. "Look at that. Look at that boy."

My old man looked at Benny but didn't say anything.

"Fifteen years old," Mr. James said. "And look at him."

Benny cried and poked in the ground with the little stick.

"Look at Max," Mr. James said. "Isn't he still breathing? Isn't he still alive? Did she eat him up?"

The tears and snot began to run out of Benny's eyes and nose. He kept jabbing the little stick down in the ground. He didn't bother to wipe his face.

"When you get tired crying, just get up from there and go inside the house," Mr. James said. "I've got all night." My old man was looking at Benny, and I knew my old man felt like walking over there and butting Benny's head against the tree two or three times. Benny was about a year older than I was and I knew if he was my old man's son, my old man would have butt his head against that tree and then picked him up and threw him in the room where Amy was. But Benny was not my old man's son, and Mr. James was not like my old man, and so Benny just sat against the tree and cried and jabbed in the ground with the little stick.

I stood up to go around the house to get some water from the well.

"Where're you going, Max?" my old man asked.

"Just to get some water," I said.

I went around the house and drew some water from the well and drank. When I came back to the porch, Benny was still sitting against the tree. He had stopped crying.

"You're ready to go in there, now?" Mr. James asked.

Benny started crying again. He still had the little stick in his hand.

My old man looked at Benny, then he looked at me.

"Well, we might as well move along," he said, picking up the string of fishes. "You're taking off now, George?"

"Might as well," Mr. James said, and stood up.

Mr. James looked at Benny sitting against the tree with his head down, then picked up his string of fishes. He and my old man started out of the yard. I went to the tree where Benny was.

"You're going, now, Benny?" I asked him.

Benny didn't look up. I stood there about a minute looking down at him, and he didn't look up once.

"Well, I'd better be going," I said. "I'll have to clean the fishes for supper."

I caught up with my old man and Mr. James and we walked down the road without saying anything.

When we had gone about a half of a mile, Mr. James looked over his shoulder and saw Benny following us.

"Damn it," Mr. James said. "This is one day that boy is going to do what I say."

Mr. James turned around and started up the road toward Benny. Benny saw him coming and stopped.

Mr. James walked up to Benny and grabbed him by the arm and turned him around. We were too far to hear if Benny was crying or not, but within myself I knew he was crying.

My old man and I started walking again.

"I guess you think you're a man, now?" my old man said.

"Sir?"

"You heard me," my old man said.

"No, sir," I said. "I don't think I'm a man."

"Well, you are," my old man said.

I didn't say anything, and my old man didn't say any more. The sun was going down, and the cool dust felt good under my bare feet.

BOY IN THE DOUBLE-BREASTED SUIT

Before I could see what had made the noise I saw my old man still holding on to the piece of chicken, and again "pow," and my old man dropped the piece of chicken on the platter, still shocked, and the preacher lowered his head a little more because all the time it was lowered a little, and commenced blessing the food, saying, "Gracious Master, we thank thee for this food which is prepared for us, the nurses of our bodies, for Christ sake, we pray, amen." Then he raised his head and looked at my old man, and got himself a piece of chicken off the platter, and passed the platter around to Mrs. Adele, right in front of my face, but Mrs. Adele passed it over to my old man, and he took off a piece, then he passed it back to her and she let me take off a piece by myself, and smiled her very wonderful way of smiling at me, then she took off a piece and we began to eat, trying not to look at my old man because he was still red where the preacher had hit him twice on the hand when he had reached for a piece of chicken without first saying his blessing.

"I suppose that hurt you," the preacher said, putting a spoonful of potato salad in his mouth and looking at my old man at the same time.

My old man didn't answer the preacher, but I knew he was mad, because nobody ever hit him and got away with it. Sitting there, I wondered if that preacher knew how lucky he was, being a preacher and not just an ordinary man.

"Now suppose the Good Lord struck you," the preacher said. "You know how much more it would hurt."

But my old man still didn't say anything and he didn't eat, and didn't move either for that much. But the preacher kept on talking, and putting chicken in his mouth, and tearing it away from the bone, and chewing; then putting the bone half covered with chicken back in his mouth, and pulling the bone out of his mouth, very clean and white like it had been washed in a stream, clean of everything.

The preacher was a tall man, and wore a black suit with a long black coat and always had a wide-rim black hat, and carried a gold chain over his chest, hooked into a buttonhole and the other end in his vest pocket, hooked onto a big watch that you could hear ticking if you sat ten feet away from him. He had very big wrinkled hands, and you could see the big veins on back of his hands and up his arms. He had eyes that set far back in his face, close-together eyes, gray eyes, and his teeth that looked almost like horse teeth were very strong, and it was said around Wakeville that he could pick up a fifty-pound sack of rice with his teeth and swing it like a pendulum for a minute every weekday, and go to church on Sunday and preach two full hours without stopping as long as the sisters of the church kept wiping his face with the towel and supplying him with ice water.

The preacher—his name was Reverend Johnson—had a little grayish-color-looking church about a mile from where Mrs. Adele lived, and Mrs. Adele and I used to go there every Sunday to Sunday school and church.

This relationship between Mrs. Adele and me came about something like this. Mom died when I was no more than seven, and about a year later my old man began to feel lonely for a lady, and he also wanted someone to kind of look after me. So he met Mrs. Adele, who was a widow, and Mrs. Adele liked him very much because he was big and strong and could cut lots of wood and make grocery for her and do all the other little chores around a house that ladies oughtn't have to do. And she liked me, too, because I looked so much like Oscar—that's my old man—as she put it, and she told me she would teach me how to keep my shirt inside my pants and keep my face clean and if I was a good little boy she would buy me a double-breasted suit with long pant legs, and I could stay with her sometimes.

So she and my old man started getting along pretty good, and my old man would take me over there on Saturday afternoon for me to stay with her all night Saturday and then he would come and get me on Sunday evening late, after church, and take me back home until the next Saturday. Mrs. Adele and I were getting along all right, too, and about two Saturdays later when I got there she showed me a long box and told me to look inside of it, and when I saw the double-breasted blue suit I ran to her and threw my arms around her and kissed her, and she smiled and hugged me and told me to go put it on.

I did, and she and my old man liked it because it was a perfect fit, and she told me to go walk around in the road in it to show it off, and I did and when I came back I saw her and my old man lying across the bed playing with each other, and I was so happy I started crying. My old man got mad and wanted to whip me because he thought I had sneaked in on them, but Mrs. Adele wouldn't let him whip me, and she told me that she and my old man were going to be married one day and she was going to be my stepmother, and I felt so good that I ran over to her and cried some more. But my old man didn't like to see me crying, and he told me to take off my double-breasted suit, and put on my old clothes and go out into the yard or somewhere in the road and play with the other children.

Though their wedding day didn't come off as soon as I thought it ought to, that didn't stop me from going over there every Saturday and going to Sunday school and church with Mrs. Adele every Sunday. We would walk side by side in the middle of the road, because the sidewalk was too grassy, and every once in a while she would look at me and smile and I would look at her and grin, and she would lay her hand on my shoulder and I would feel so good. And at the church all the people would meet her and talk to her and say what a nice-looking young man I was in my double-breasted blue suit, and she would feel so proud of me, and then we would go inside and sit down and listen to the preacher preach and beat on the big Bible with both fists, and I would ask her why he was beating on the Bible and hollering and she would nod her head and tell me I oughtn't talk in church but pay attention and listen so I could be a good boy. So I would sit there and try to listen and try to make out what he was saying, but all the time not being able to because he was making too much noise, and soon I would find myself yawning out loud.

Then after church Mrs. Adele would talk with the preacher awhile, and they would wander on my old man's name and saying what a nice young man I was, and wouldn't it be great if all three of us could come to church together; and then she would talk with some other people who kept a little girl with them, and all the time she would be feeling so proud of me, and they would be so proud of her for bringing me to church and soon getting married herself, and while they would be up there talking I would be trying to figure out a way to get that little old funny-looking girl around the church somewhere so I could yank her hair or do her something, but she would never follow me, being smart, and just stand there with her little old freckled face, her legs crossed, and looking at me. Then Mrs. Adele and I would walk home to her house and wait for my old man, and then we would all eat supper together, and then my old man and I would start out for home across the fields, and not get there till way up in the night.

"The Lord is good," the preacher said. "If He was only like man."

"Amen," Mrs. Adele said.

I looked at Mrs. Adele because I had never heard her say amen in the house before and something kind of slipped out of my mouth—I don't know what—and my old man looked at me and said, "What's that you said, Max? Now don't you start."

"I didn't say anything."

"You should be proud of him," the preacher said. "But ashamed of yourself."

"I've got nothing to be ashamed of, preacher," my old man said, and for the first time he took a bite off the piece of chicken.

"What?" the preacher said. "You mean to sit there and say you're not ashamed of your sins?"

My old man ate and didn't say anything else to the preacher.

"I'm talking to you, Oscar Wheeler," the preacher said, rolling his eyes at my old man.

My old man kept on eating.

The preacher stuck his tongue down in the corner of his mouth, between his back teeth and his jaw, and dugged out a piece of chicken that he hadn't swallowed, and chewed on it and all the time looking straight at my old man.

"Well, if you've got nothing to be sorry about, I'm sorry for you," the preacher said. And when my old man didn't say anything, the preacher struck his big fist on the table and made a loud noise.

My old man looked at the preacher, yet didn't say anything. But if you knew my old man like I did, you could tell by his eyes that he wanted to say, "Don't knock on that table like that. You can talk to me without beating on the table, can't you? I ain't deaf, and I'm right here." But he didn't say this and he and the preacher just looked into each other's eyes until my old man finally bit off the chicken again.

"I suppose you put him up to this," my old man said, looking at Mrs. Adele.

Mrs. Adele looked down at the table. I felt sorry for her.

"Well, neither one of you'll have to worry about my sins after today," he said.

Mrs. Adele raised her head and looked at him, and I looked at him and I was wondering if my old man was thinking about going off someplace—or maybe shoot himself like Mr. Robbins had done because he had so many children.

"I won't be coming back," he said.

"You don't mean that, Oscar," Mrs. Adele said.

"I like Mrs. Adele."

"You keep out of this, Max," my old man said.

"Run, sinner, run," the preacher said.

My old man looked at the preacher, then he reached over and got another piece of chicken from the platter. Mrs. Adele wanted to hold the platter up so he could get more than one piece, but my old man didn't want but one piece then, or if he did, he was going to show Mrs. Adele that he was mad with her, too.

"You think running going to do any good?" the preacher said. "Can't the Good Lord find you no matter where you run or hide?"

"Can't you shut him up?"

"Sure," the preacher said. "Sure, shut up the word of the Lord."

My old man didn't hit the preacher like he wanted to, but kept on eating the piece of chicken. He was holding the drumstick with both hands. He had to know where both his hands were all the time, or he might've accidentally hit the preacher. And though he wasn't a churchgoing man, preachers were the only type of people I had never seen my old man take a swing at.

"I thought it was best, Oscar," Mrs. Adele said. "Like you, Max, and me all together."

"I'll do my own thinking from now on," my old man said.

"Pa—"

"Shut up, Max."

"Yes, sir."

"You just can't reason with some people," the preacher said. He looked at my old man awhile, then he looked at Mrs. Adele. "For your sake, Adele, I'm sorry."

"Don't give up, Reverend Johnson," she said.

"I'm not giving up," the preacher said. "I'm just sorry for you."

"Go take off your suit, Max," my old man said.

"Sir?"

"You heard me."

"I don't want to take it off."

"I said take it off," my old man roared.

"What are you making him take it off for?" Mrs. Adele asked.

"He's leaving it," my old man said.

"I want my double-breasted suit."

"Didn't you hear me?" my old man said.

"This is between you and me, Oscar," Mrs. Adele said. "And I won't allow you to take it out on that child."

My old man gave me one of those looks that I knew what it meant, and I went around the table and stood in the door, looking at the three of them. I could feel the hot tears coming into my eyes.

"I don't want to take off my suit, Pa."

"Well, you're going to," he said. "'And hurry up about it. I want to get home before dark."

"Oscar," Mrs. Adele said; she was almost crying. "Please."

But my old man just looked at me, and I knew there was no use, and I went to the room that I stayed in when I was at Mrs. Adele's house. I sat on the bed, and I could feel a big lump in my throat, and I wanted to cry, but couldn't, then Mrs. Adele came into the room and knelt down in front of me and hugged me and I hugged her and we both cried.

Then she stopped and kissed me on both cheeks, and I saw where the tears had run down her face. She wiped her eyes on a little pocket handkerchief, then she wiped mine and held the little hand-kerchief up to my nose and told me to blow, but nothing came out, and she wiped my eyes again.

"You're not acting like a big boy," she said.

"I thought you were going to be my stepmother."

"Still am," she said.

"No," I said. "Pa'll never come back."

She smiled and nodded her head. "He will," she said.

"I hope so, Mrs. Adele," I said. "I want you to be my stepmother so bad. And you all were getting along so good before that—before today."

She hugged me, then when I started to unbutton my suit coat, she stood up to get my clothes off the nail that was back of the door, and she was going to leave the room till I had changed clothes so she wouldn't have to look at me.

Just when she was getting ready to reach for the clothes, we heard *ka-bung*, and we ran out of the room into the kitchen and I saw my old man getting off the floor, and the preacher standing beside the table with his long arms and big fists hanging to his side. I didn't know how it had happened, but that preacher must've hit my old man when he wasn't looking, but my old man was getting off the floor when we got to the kitchen and he was going to tear into the preacher if Mrs. Adele hadn't started screaming.

"Don't you hit a man of God, Oscar Wheeler," she screamed. "Don't you hit a man of God."

She stood between my old man and the preacher with them glaring at each other, then my old man raised his hand and felt his jaw like he was trying to reset it. He looked at the preacher again, then he jerked away and went out on the little back porch.

"I'm sorry, Adele," the preacher said. Then he looked up at the ceiling and said a low prayer that nobody could hear but himself. After that he got his hat. "Sometimes you got to play by the other fellow's rules to get results."

"No, Reverend Johnson," Mrs. Adele said Christian-like.

He patted her on the shoulder.

"You're a good Christian, Adele," the preacher said. He glanced over his shoulder at my old man on the back porch, then he looked at me. "Keep up the good work, young man."

I didn't know what he was talking about, but I nodded my head. He came over to me and put his hand on my shoulder, then he walked out of the house, very straight and tall and looking directly ahead.

"Go take off your suit, Max," Mrs. Adele said. "I want to talk to your father."

I went back to the room and took off the suit and folded the trousers and hung it on a clothes hanger. I put on my blue shirt and my dirty overalls, and Mrs. Adele came back into the room and said, "Surprise for you, Max."

"Ma'am?"

"You can take your suit home with you."

"Pa said so?"

"Uh-huh."

I felt like running out to the back porch and kissing my old man, but he might've still been mad at that preacher and took a poke at me. So I didn't go out there where he was, but got the box that I had brought the suit to Mrs. Adele's house in. Mrs. Adele took the suit off the hanger for me and folded it neatly and put it in the box. When she closed the box she sat on the bed and looked at me.

"Max?"

"Ma'am?"

"I want you to do something for me."

"Yes, ma'am?"

"I want you to always remember that I want to be your—your stepmother, hear?"

I looked down at the floor. "Yes, ma'am."

She took me by the hand and brought me closer to her.

"You want me to be, don't you?"

"Yes, ma'am."

She put her hand under my chin and raised my head.

"If you wish hard enough it still might happen," she said, trying to look in my eyes, and me trying not to look in hers, because all the time I was afraid I might start crying again.

"Max," my old man called.

"Coming, Pa."

Mrs. Adele was still holding my hand.

"And I want you to keep saying your prayers, hear?"

"Yes, ma'am."

"And who are you going to pray for?" she said, a little jollylike.

"For you and for Pa—and for everybody."

"But your father more."

I nodded.

Then she hugged me real hard, and when she released me she pushed the box toward me, but all the time keeping her head turned away from me so I couldn't see that she was crying.

"'Bye, Mrs. Adele," I said at the door.

But she didn't look at me, and when my old man heard me coming he walked down the steps, and me, with the double-breasted suit tucked under my arms, I followed him.

Mary Louise

I

The sun hadn't rised yet, but I wasn't going to sleep no more, and I thought the best thing for me to do was to get up. I pushed the sheet back and sat on the side of the bed a minute. Then I said to myself, Sitting here ain't going to get the work done. And I got up and put on a dress and went back in the kitchen. It didn't have any water in the pail, and I got it and carried it on to the pump. Across the stream it was red 'cause the sun was just getting ready to come up. The morning was still a little cool, and the grass was still wet from the dew last night. Over 'cross the fence I saw Mr. Richard coming out of his kitchen with a bucket of slop, and I could hear the hogs running 'cross the lot to meet him.

Farther on up the nook I could hear Mrs. Olive Jarreau calling her chickens to feed 'em, and the next second I could hear her hollering at St. John's dog. She was telling the dog she couldn't even feed her chickens in peace if he wasn't 'round there swallowing up everything fast as it hit the ground. She was telling the dog he was more trifling than his master, and one day his old trifling master was going to come there and find his old trifling dog stretched out on his gallery dead as a doornail. She hollered at the dog again, and then she must've picked up something and threw it at him 'cause I heard the dog running 'cross the yard howling.

I took the pail of water in the house and poured up some in the washbasin. After I had washed, I put some corncobs in the stove and lit the fire. By the time Dad come back in the kitchen I had already gone to my room and made up my bed and swept the floor, and had come back in the kitchen to start the breakfast. When I heard him coming back there I pulled the skillet over the front burner to fry the two pieces of salt meat I already had in there. Dad went in the back awhile, and then he came inside to wash up. After he got through he sat at the table, and I brought him his food. When everything was on the table I went to my room to stay there till he was gone. I knowed if I had stayed back there he was going to say something 'bout Jackson again, and God knows I didn't want to hear no more of his squabbling.

I got my little hand mirror and my comb and went over to the window. I passed the comb through my hair a long time, just to while away the time. Then when I heard him leaving the house I put the things up and went back in the kitchen to cook my own breakfast.

II

Aunt Vivian had told me anytime I wanted to come to the city she would help me to find some kind of job. Right then I couldn't make up my mind to go or to stay. I wanted to go, and I didn't want to go. If I went and left him there I was sure to lose, then. But if I stayed, there was always a chance. The reason was I just couldn't see Jackson loving Lillian. She was pretty and all that, yes, but I couldn't see him loving her. There wasn't a thing to her. Nothing but face and hair, and I didn't think Jackson was that kind. I didn't think he was that kind, and I didn't care what they said, I wasn't going to ever think it. If he had told me himself he loved her, then I would think it. But till then I wasn't going to. I saw him going over there, but that didn't mean nothing. He could've been just going over there to talk to Mrs. Della or Catherine. I didn't see him and Lillian walking together like Emmy said they had been doing. I knowed Emmy was jealous of him. Even from the first day he was back there, she started putting all that stuff on her face to make him look at her. Then when he didn't pay her no mind she tried to get something up on him. I knowed her too well to go 'round believing everything she said.

Because even when he was small he used to go over there. Lillian wasn't there then, but he used to go over there. I used to tell on him. Sometimes I wouldn't, but sometimes I'd tell soon's I seen him running 'cross that pasture. And what Miss Charlotte used to put on him nothing could take it off. Remember the time she whipped both me and him for going up in that loft. That was the worst whipping I ever got in my life. It was in this same house. Right there in Dad's room. Me, him, Brother, Nancy—a bunch of us here that day. Then Nancy, she wanted to do something else 'sides just playing jacks. She wanted to play Mama and Papa. I knowed all the time what she was getting next to, and I kept on saying over and over, "No, Nancy, that's a sin. We can't do that."

And her, "That ain't no sin. You just trying to be nicey-nicey, you."

And I said, "It's a sin. That's what they say."

And she said, "I don't care what they say. It ain't no sin."

"It is," I said.

"It ain't," she said.

"It is," I said.

"All right, Miss Nicey-Nicey," she said, "if it's a sin for you it ain't none for me and I'm going to do it much as I want."

"If you do it with Jackson I'll tell, too," I said. "You see if I don't tell, too."

And she said, "You do and I never stop beating you, too. You just do and see if I ever stop beating on you."

And him and Brother and the rest of 'em was playing out in the yard. What was they playing? Must've been playing marbles. It had to be marbles, 'cause they was always playing marbles. And she went out there where they was and asked 'em if they wanted to play hiding in the house, and they came on in and they went hiding and I couldn't find 'em for nothing.

I found Brother and the other children right away, but couldn't find him and Skinny Nancy for nothing. I gave up and told 'em to come out 'cause I couldn't find 'em, but they didn't come out. Then after a long time both of 'em came creeping out from where they was. Then Skinny Nancy had to look for us, and I seen him going up the loft and I followed him up the loft, and he thought I was Brother. I still remember him saying, "That you, Brother?"

"That's me," I said.

"What you doing up here?" he said.

"I'm hiding up here."

"Well, you don't make no noise," he said. "You know how you like to make noise."

"I ain't going to make none," I said.

And I crawled over where he was, and he was breathing hard, and I was breathing hard, too, 'cause I was tired from climbing up the wall in the loft.

"How come I couldn't find y'all?" I said.

"Shhhh," he said.

"Hanh, how come?" I said.

"Shhhh," he said.

And I started crying.

"How come?" I said. "How come I couldn't find y'all?"

"They going to hear you, you keep that noise up," he said.

"How come? What y'all was doing, Jackson?" I said.

"Shhhh," he said. "Don't make no noise."

"What y'all was doing?" I said.

"Nothing," he said.

"Yeah, y'all was doing something," I said. "Y'all was sinning. That's what y'all was doing."

"We wasn't sinning," he said.

"Yes, y'all was," I said. "Y'all was sinning."

"No, we wasn't," he said. "She wanted to make me sin but I didn't. She held me down and tried to make me sin with her but I wouldn't."

"How come you didn't holler, then?" I said.

"How can you holler with somebody laying on top your mouth, hanh?"

"You didn't sin with her none?" I said.

"I told you I didn't, didn't I?" he said.

And I stopped crying and just sat there looking at him. "How come?" I said.

He didn't answer.

"Hanh?"

He still didn't answer me.

"Hanh, Jackson?" I said.

"I don't like old Skinny Nancy, that's why I didn't sin with her," he said. "Now, you stop bothering me."

And I felt good and we was quiet and I heard him breathing 'cause he was still tired and I was breathing hard 'cause I had climbed up that wall and I was tired and it was dark in there and it was hot in there and I heard him breathing 'cause I was right up against him.

"Jackson?" I said.

"Hanh?" he said.

And I didn't say nothing 'cause I was scared, and a little bit later I said, "You want to sin with me?"

"I don't know," he said.

We was quiet again. And I said, "Jackson?"

"What this time?" he said.

"You ever seen anybody sinning?"

"Yeah," he said. "One time I seen Joe and Veta."

I always remember he said Joe and Veta, 'cause Joe and Veta got married when they growed up; and I always remember he said Joe and Veta. Just like that he said Joe and Veta. Right under that same house Joe and 'em used to live in.

"What they was doing?" I said.

"Sinning," he said.

"I mean how," I said.

"He was laying on top of her," he said.

"Oh, that's all sinning is?"

"I reckon so," he said. "I don't know."

We was quiet and we listened, but we didn't bear nobody coming.

"They never find us up here," he said. And we was quiet again.

"You want to sin?" he said.

"I don't know."

And we was quiet a long time and we listened and we didn't hear nobody coming.

"You think it'll be all right?" I said. "Nobody'll come up here and catch us?"

"I don't know," he said.

"I want if you want," I said.

"You want to?" he said.

"If you want to," I said.

"First you got to lay back on your back then," he said. I did and I stretched out my legs and I felt him.

"Wait," he said.

"Hanh?" I said.

"We got to do this," he said. "Hold still."

We didn't a bit more know what we was doing 'an a man in the moon. And once there I opened my eyes and looked at him and he was looking at me like he was thinking the same thing. Then he laid down 'side me and then every few minutes he passed his tongue over my face, and every time he did it to me I did it back to him. Over and over and over.

"Like me to do that?" he said.

"Uh-huh. You like me to do it to you?"

"Uh-huh."

"Let's come up here and do it all the time," I said.

"Sinning, too?" he said.

"You like to sin?" I said.

"Uh-huh," he said.

And he passed his tongue over my face and under my neck and I started laughing, and I quit and did him that and he started laughing. Then he quit laughing and did it to me, and I laughed again. And then the trapdoor shot up and they said, "There they is. Just like Skinny Nancy said."

"Bring 'em down here," Miss Charlotte said. "And Jackson better not run. I mean he better not run. Bring 'em down here."

They grabbed us by the ankles and dragged us to that trapdoor and started dropping us to the floor like we was sacks of potatoes. Somebody was there to catch me, but nobody caught him and he hit the floor. She grabbed my ear and grabbed him and started up the road with us, with a big drove of 'em following behind and more coming out on the gallery to watch us go by. And me hollering there like I was crazy, and him not hollering at all but just doing all his might to get loose. She had a good grip on both of us—but that still didn't keep him from trying, or keep me from hollering, "I got a splinter in my tail, I got a splinter in my tail, I got a splinter in my tail, I want that splinter out my tail." And just hollering:

"I want that splinter out, I want that splinter out, I want that splinter out my tail." But her never saying a word—just carrying us by our ears. And me just a-hollering, and him over there still trying to break loose. Jerking and jerking and jerking, and me just hollering. When she got to the house, she made three of 'em hold him 'cause two couldn't, 'cause he kept hitting and kicking every time they got close. Then three of 'em jumped on him and held him down.

"All right, miss," she said. "Come on and get yours first."

I started hollering louder: "You going to whip me and I got a splinter in my tail, I want that splinter out my tail."

"All right," she said. "Where it at, and there better be one, and a good one, too, if you know what's good for you. Point to it. Touch the spot."

"It hurt if I touch it," I said.

"Point then," she said.

"Right there," I said, pointing. "See it?"

"All right," she said. "It's a little one, but I'll get it out. One of y'all standing 'round there find me a needle. Heaten it and bring it back here when it's cold so I can get the splinter out. But that ain't going to keep the strop off your tail, miss. I'm going to give you something today you going to remember the rest of your life. Ain't big enough to wipe your nose and you laying up in the loft. I fix you. If y'all knowed what y'all was doing it'd be something else. But you don't know. Hurry up and bring me that needle. I want give 'em their medicine 'fore they forget what they getting it for."

That was the worst whipping I ever got in my life, and his was worser 'cause he wouldn't cry. And that was one thing 'bout them old people: if you didn't cry they beat you till the sun went down. And if it was already down they beat you till it come up again. They made you cry, all right. After a while you was glad to cry.

The thing me and him done gone through when we was small can't be changed by something like Lillian. I ain't going to believe he love Lillian till he tell me he love her. When he do, I'll believe him. But if he don't, I'll never believe it. They can say just what they want to say. I don't care.

III

I got the broom and went outside to sweep the gallery off. I didn't have to go up to the big house till I got ready, and I thought after I had swept off the gallery I'd go up to Dora till I got ready to go to work. When I came outside I saw Jackson coming down the road. I thought he was going to Madame Bayonne's house, but when he passed it I figured him and Brother had somewhere to go and he was going down there to see if Brother was ready. Then when he got in front of our house he turned and came up the walk. He hadn't seen me yet and I ran inside and stuck the broom in a corner and pulled off the apron I was wearing. But I had to be doing something when he came in. I got a dishrag and took a stack of plates out of the safe and started wiping 'em out. I heard him come up on the gallery and knock on the door, and I told him to come in.

"Hi, what you know?" he said, coming back in the kitchen.

"Nothing," I said.

"I see you're busy," he said.

"Just thought I'd clean up some," I said. "Can I get you a chair to sit down?"

"No, I'd rather stand," he said, and went to the back door, where it was more cooler. "It's going to be hot again today."

"Yeah, once this heat start setting in."

"Where's Herb?" he asked.

"Working."

"Don't you go to work today?"

"Yeah, but I don't go till late," I said. "All I have to do is make a cake today. And I don't have to go till I get ready."

He turned and looked outside, and his back was to me. He was wearing a brown shirt and a pair of brown pants. The shirt had short sleeves, but he still had 'em rolled up some.

I wiped the plate and put it in the safe. And I got another one and started wiping it out.

"How's Miss Charlotte?"

"Okay," he said, looking out in the yard. I knowed he was looking at all the weeds we had out there, and I had asked Dad a hundred times to chop 'em down. I had kept the little ones down 'side the walk back there, but I wasn't going to hurt myself trying to chop down them big weeds. That was a man's job.

I carried the plate to the safe, and I got one more and wiped it out. When I finished this, I folded the rag and stuck it in the safe drawer. Jackson heard me pushing the drawer, and he glanced over his shoulder.

"Finished work?" he said, smiling.

"Yes."

"Would you like to go for a walk somewhere?" he asked. "I would like to talk to you."

"All right."

I went to my room to get my hat. He owe me some kind of expla-nation for all he been doing, I thought in there, and this walk I been waiting for since he been here. I thank God it done come at last.

I put my hat on and went back to the kitchen where he was.

He glanced at my hat when I came back in there, and then we left. I wanted all of 'em to see us together, now, and soon as we went out the gate I saw Nancy deRogers come out on her gallery to watch us. And I saw Emmy peeping from behind a curtain at us when we was passing by their place. But she didn't come out on the gallery the way Nancy did. When we got down to Mr. James Martin, Mrs. Sarah was sitting out on the gallery shelling a pan of beans. She raised her arm to wave at us. We waved back. She asked Jackson how Miss Charlotte was. Jackson said she was all right.

"That's good," Mrs. Sarah said. "I'll probably go up there after I get dinner done." That was the last house along the stream, and after we passed it we was back in the field. There wasn't any trees here, like there was along the stream. There was just sugarcane on both side of us. The sugarcane went so far, and then you came to corn, and then to cotton. On the other side of the cotton was the pasture where Mr. Boudreau and 'em kept their cattles. They had trees along the pasture, and I reckoned that's where we was going. I tried to think what he wanted to talk to me 'bout. Just last night I seen him going over there, and he knowed I seen him, so what it was he wanted to talk 'bout? Did he want to tell me to keep out his business? I didn't think that was it, 'cause look to me like if that was it, he would've been mad when he came to the house. But he wasn't mad at all. Just the other way 'round.

I didn't know what he had on his mind, but this was my chance, and I was going to speak my piece today. I was going to ask all the questions I had been storing up and I was going to tell him what I thought. I just wanted the Lord to give me strength, and I was going to speak my piece.

I hoped what he had to say was something good, and if it was, soons I went back, I was going straight to old Emmy and tell her all 'bout it. Just day 'fore yesterday she was saying he wasn't this, he wasn't that; and I was a fool for being that way 'bout him. I sure felt good when I passed by there and seen her peeping from behind that curtain. She thought nobody seen her there, but I did. I knowed she was going to be there, and that's why I made it my business to look that way when we was passing.

I bet you her and Nancy deRogers was going to have a big talk 'bout what happened. I could just hear 'em right now. I bet you she had already gone over to Nancy's house.

Well, let 'em talk all they wanted. I wanted to be looking in her face when I told her he proposed to me. That would be something. I bet you her mouth'd fall open a foot. And then me and him'd go to Bayonne and get the ring. And every time I seen her in the road I'd flash it in her face. I'd be the happiest person in the world if that's what it was. I'd show it to every last one of 'em. All of 'em. Everyone who been saying I'm a fool. Dad, 'specially. I'd show it to him every time he looked my way. I'd keep it shiny and every time he looked at me it'd be flashing.

I ought to not get my hopes up that high, I thought. It could've been anything. It didn't have to be a proposal. Maybe he wanted to ask me if I wanted to go to Bayonne to a show, or maybe he wanted to ask me if I want to go to New Orleans one day with him and Brother. But if it was no more 'an that, he could've asked me that at home, couldn't he? Did he have to come way across here for that? It must've been something big he wanted to say. Something—and he didn't want to be stopped with somebody running in the house. But I better stop thinking 'bout it, I thought. I'd find out soon enough.

IV

"That looks like a good place to sit down," Jackson said.

We'd turned off the road and went over to the tree, and he took out his pocket handkerchief and spread it out on the ground for me to sit on.

"No. You," I said.

"These things are already dirty," he said. "Sitting on the ground can't make them look any worse."

"They look all right," I said.

"That's because of the shade," he said. "You can't see the dirt in the shade."

I sat on the handkerchief and spread out my dress. I was wearing a white dress with lots of big flowers in it. I think it was Miss Charlotte who had give me the cloth. And I had made the dress myself.

When I sat down, Jackson moved back and sat against the tree.

"Watch for ants, there," I said.

Jackson leaned forward and looked at the tree, and then he leaned back 'gainst it again.

"None," he said, stretching out his legs and looking at me. I looked over at him, and then I looked down the field like I saw something down there I was interested in. There wasn't nothing down there, but I just couldn't look at him when he was looking at me like that. If he wasn't I could look at him all day, 'cause I like to look at him. But I couldn't look at him at all if he was looking at me at the same time.

"Why haven't you gotten married?" he said.

"Me?" I said.

"Yes," he said.

"Never found nobody," I said.

"Why not?"

"I don't know," I said.

"Did you look for somebody?"

"I guess not."

"You can't find anyone unless you look for him."

"How come you ain't married?" I said, looking at him.

"Oh, I'm married," he said.

"You married?" I said.

"Of course."

"When you got married?" I said.

Jackson laughed, and I laughed, too. I thought he was really telling me the truth.

"No, I'm not married," he said.

"How come?"

"I never found anyone I would like to be married to."

"Lillian's there," I said. And I looked at him to see what he was going to say to that.

"I'm afraid I'm not Lillian's kind, as far as marriage goes. And I don't think she's my kind either—as far as marriage goes."

"You don't love her?"

"No," he said.

"What you go over there for, then?"

"Where else can you go 'round here?"

"It got other places to go to."

"Name one," he said.

"They got Bayonne, there," I said.

"I don't like Bayonne," he said.

They sure got more there 'an they got over here, I said to myself.

"You ever go to Bayonne?" he asked.

"Sometimes."

"With your boyfriend?"

"By myself," I said. "I don't have a boyfriend."

"Why not?"

"I just don't have one," I said.

"You mean you don't have one now?"

"I never had one," I said.

"Come, now."

"None I cared for."

"But you did have some."

"I didn't care for any of 'em," I said.

"Not one?"

"No," I said. "Not one of 'em."

A bird flew from 'cross the pasture and lit on one of the cotton stalks. He hit the stalk pretty hard, and it bent forward with him. Look like he was going to fall off, but he held on tight. But he didn't stay there for long. He just came there to rest, and then he flew away again. A green pecan fell out the tree and landed in the middle by us. I looked at it laying there in the middle, but all the time I could feel Jackson still looking at me.

"Why did you stay here, Mary Louise?" he said. "Don't you have people in the city?"

"I got some there," I said.

"Then why didn't you go to them and go on and finish school?"

"I wanted to stay here."

"Why? To work in some white woman's kitchen all your life?"

"That wasn't my reason."

"What was it?"

I raised my head and looked at him, and then I looked away again.

"Mary Louise," he said.

"What?" I said, with my head still down.

I wasn't going to look at him again, 'cause I knowed now he wasn't going to say he loved me, and he wasn't going to propose to me. He wasn't going to ask me to go to a show or to New Orleans with him. He wasn't going to ask me none of that. He just wanted me back there so he could talk to me like I was a child and he was somebody older. Like he knowed the answer to everything.

"Do you remember when we were small?"

I nodded.

"We loved each other. You remember how much we loved each other?"

"Yes."

"Then I went away. How old was I? I was twelve, wasn't I? And you were what? How old were you?"

I didn't answer him.

"Hanh?"

"I don't know. Ten, I guess."

"That's right. You were ten, and I was twelve. And that's been ten years. Ten long years. And lots of things can change in ten years. Don't you agree?"

No, I didn't agree, but I didn't say it. It hadn't changed with me, and I wasn't going to say it had, 'cause it hadn't. He wanted me to say it so his conscience would be clear, but I wasn't going to say it.

"Did you expect me to come back after ten years and pick up where we left off? Did you, Mary Louise?"

I still didn't answer him. And after that he was quiet, and just looking at me. I picked up some dirt and rubbed it between my fingers.

"It can't ever be like that again," I heard him saying.

A drop of water fell in the place where I had got the dirt from. I raised my hand and wiped my eyes, but I kept my head down all the time.

"Time changes people," he said. "Everybody changes. I expected to come back here and find you married."

"To who?" I said.

"I don't know. Somebody."

He went on, but I didn't hear him no more. I still had the dirt in my hand, and I stirred it 'round with my fingers.

At first I tried to hold my crying back, but it wasn't no use; I just let it come the way it wanted to. I wasn't shamed to cry in front of him. I had cried in front of him before; and this time was just like the others. Like we was still small, and he had never been anywhere.

He moved from 'gainst the tree and came over where I was. He started talking to me, but I didn't try to make out what he was saying. All I could think about was what a fool I had been. How right everybody else was, and how wrong I was all this time. I couldn't think of nothing else.

Did he think I liked going up to that white woman's house every day? Did he think I liked taking her 'buses? Or them white men telling me anything they wanted or pinching me ever' time they passed by? Did he think I liked that—or Dad fussing at me both night and day? And all the rest of 'em there making fun of me when there wasn't anybody else to pick on? Did he think I liked that? He put his arms 'round my shoulders and pulled me closer to him, but I knowed why he did it, and I jerked myself away.

"I don't need your pity."

"I wasn't trying to pity you."

"Take it to somebody else. Take it to them yellow bitches you like to go 'round. Just don't bring it to me."

I got to my feet and stood right over him. I hoped there was something close by I could hit him with. I couldn't see a thing, and I drawed back and hit him with my fist hard as I could. I hit him again, and I hit him again, and he didn't even try to get out my way. He just sat there with his head down, not even flinching.

I turned and started running toward the end. I was crying too hard to watch where I was going, and I stumbled and fell. I got up and started running again. I didn't know why I was running; I just had to run.

When I got to the road up by the stream I looked back, but I couldn't see him. I passed my hand over my face, and tried to look like nothing had happened back there. Mrs. Sarah looked at me when I passed by her house, but I made 'tend I didn't see her.

When I got home I went to my room and locked the door. I just wanted to be by myself so I could think what a fool I had been. All my life I had been nothing but a fool for people.

MY GRANDPA AND THE HAINT

At first it wasn't much more than a grunt. Something like—"Un-hunh." Then he was quiet. Then he did it again, twice. "Un-hunh, un-hunh." Then quiet again. Then the third time he did it he didn't even try to hold it back. He just came right out and giggled.

I'll give him twenty, I said. One, two, three, four—I got to twelve, and Pap said, "Guess that's enough for today. Catch 'em all one day, won't have nothing left to come back for."

So we pulled in our lines and went up the bank. I was carrying the string of fish, and Pap was walking in front of me with that little fishing pole over his shoulder. That little fishing pole was bent at the end, but it was strong as iron. Pap had had it ever since I could remember, and I was twelve years old then.

Just before we got to the crossroad I heard that little grunt again. Then about a half a minute later two more little grunts. Then a little while after that, the giggling. Well, that'll be another hour or so, I told myself. And when we came to the crossroad, just like I was thinking we would do, we turned toward her house. Pap was walking in front and me right behind him.

After going a little piece, I could see the trees around Miss Molly

Bee's fence. They were tall pecan and oak trees, and they hid the yard and the house from us. You didn't see the house at all till you got right on it.

Miss Molly Bee was sitting out on the gallery fanning. She was always sitting out on the gallery fanning. She was a big Creole lady with a pile of jet-black hair. She smiled as soon as she seen us coming in the yard.

"Thought you might not drop by today," she said.

Pap gave her a little smile, and she smiled back at Pap. People said she had many boyfriends, but I think she liked Pap the most. When she looked at Pap, look like there wasn't nobody else in the world.

"Hello, Bobby," she said.

"Miss Molly Bee," I said.

I laid the string of fish on the bottom step, and sat on the one just above it. Pap sat on the gallery and leaned back against the post. He never sat in a chair no matter where he went. At home Mom would try to get him to sit in a chair when they was out on the gallery together, but Pap never would. He said he believed it was the Indian in him made him sit on the floor all the time. But, anyhow, for courtesy sake, Miss Molly Bee said: "Get you a chair, Toddy?" Pap's name was Robert, same as mine, but Miss Molly Bee called him Toddy. She had made up that little name herself.

"Good right here," Pap said. "Ooooo, it's been hot."

"Sure has," Miss Molly Bee said. "Got some lemonade inside. Get you a glassful?"

"That would be fine," Pap said. Pap was always sporty when he talked to Miss Molly Bee.

"Little Bobby?" Miss Molly Bee said.

"Yes, ma'am. Thank you," I said.

So she went in and got it, and we sat there drinking and keeping very quiet. Then after a little while, I could feel it was a little too quiet. I could feel it was about time for one of them to grunt. I raised the glass and took a swallow. Nothing. I lowered the glass. Still nothing. Nothing but quiet. What the heck's going on? I said to myself.

I was just about ready to raise the glass for the last few drops when I heard Miss Molly Bee go, "Un-hunh." Pap waited about a minute and then he went like that, too, "Un-hunh." Then it was quiet a while and then Miss Molly Bee went like that again—twice. Then Pap went like that twice. Then it was quiet a minute, and then Miss Molly Bee started giggling very softly. And just when she was getting ready to quit, Pap started his giggling.

"Hen still laying up the road?" Pap asked Miss Molly Bee.

And I said to myself, You might as well stand up right now and head on up there, 'cause that's where you'll be going in about two minutes from now.

"Still laying up there," Miss Molly Bee said. "Won't break habit for nothing."

"Picked your eggs today?" Pap asked.

"Not yet," Miss Molly Bee said.

It was quiet a minute. Then Pap said, "Bobby, why 'on't you up there and get Miss Molly Bee them eggs?"

"Maybe it's too hot, Toddy," Miss Molly Bee said.

"No, ma'am. It's not too hot," I said.

I stood up to leave. But before I went down the steps, I looked at Pap. One day, I said to myself. One day—just watch. I'm getting sick and tired of hunting these eggs every time I go fishing. I left them sitting there on the gallery. But I knowed five minutes later they was going to be back in the kitchen, and Miss Molly Bee was going to have her foot in that basin of water.

The first time I went over there with Pap, they started that giggling just like they did today. That was about a year ago. One of them giggle a little while, then the other one giggle a little while. Then one, then the other. Then they started talking about that hen nest way up the road. I said I would go and get the eggs if Miss Molly

Bee didn't mind. She said No, she would be obliged if I did, and she told Pap to point out the spot for me. Pap stood up to point it out, and he told me while I was up there I could break me a piece of cane or pick me some pecans since it wasn't necessary for me to hurry right back. I didn't know what he was getting to, so I tore up there and got the eggs and tore right back. They wasn't on the gallery where I'd left 'em, but as I started 'round the house I could hear Miss Molly Bee giggling. I didn't know what she was giggling about, and since I was a little boy, it sure wasn't any of my business. So instead of going back there where they was, I went back to the front and sat on the steps. As I went by the door I could see her sitting in a chair way back in the kitchen, and I could see she had her foot in a wash-basin. I couldn't see Pap at all, but I figured that since Miss Molly Bee was giggling like that, Pap must to have been somewhere around. I sat on the step waiting for them. Then when they was through doing what they was doing back there, both of 'em came to the front. I gave Miss Molly Bee the egg, and then me and Pap left.

The next time we went fishing, Pap started that giggling at the bayou again. Then a few minutes later, me and him was leaving. When we came up to the crossroad we turned left. Then the same old thing all over. Miss Molly Bee asked us if we wanted some lemonade and we said yes. Then after we had been there a little while, her and Pap started that giggling. Giggle little while, then the hen nest came up. Hen nest came up, then I had to go looking for eggs.

"Get yourself a piece of cane while you up there," Pap said. "You can sit under that pecan tree and eat it. Good shade up there."

But the second day I didn't want any cane either. And when I got back to the house, both of 'em was back in the kitchen again. I could hear Miss Molly Bee giggling a mile.

The third time I said I was going to find out more about all this giggling. So instead of coming back through the front, I came back the other way. Miss Molly Bee had plenty weeds back there in her yard, so I could hide myself pretty good. I had just got myself settled when they came back in the kitchen. Pap had the basin of water, and Miss Molly Bee had the chair. Pap set the basin on the floor, and Miss Molly Bee sat in her chair and stuck her foot in it. Then Pap went to work. He rolled up both his sleeves and started washing Miss Molly Bee's foot. At first he was washing it very slowly, and at first Miss Molly Bee was giggling just a little bit. Then as Pap started working a little higher, round the ankle, Miss Molly Bee started laughing a little more. And when he got around the calf of Miss Molly Bee's leg, and started playing with her calf, and making it shake and all that, Miss Molly Bee really started laughing. For a second there I thought she was going to take with a fit she was laughing so much. But Pap stopped just in time, and a minute later Miss Molly Bee had stopped laughing, too. . . . But that was only one leg. Pap had to do the same thing on the other one. So again, Miss Molly Bee started giggling real slowly. Then when Pap really started shaking her calf, she started laughing harder and harder. But one thing about Pap, he knew when to stop. He knew how to keep Miss Molly Bee from laughing too much where she might hurt herself.

So after he had washed both of her legs, she gave him the towel, and he dried 'em for her. Then she stuck her leg way out and worked her toes. Then I saw Pap take her leg in both arms, like you take a chunk of wood, and kiss Miss Molly Bee right on the knee. Well, look at Pap, will you, I said to myself. Then Miss Molly Bee stuck out her other leg and worked her toes on that foot, and Pap took it and kissed that knee. After this was all done with, Pap pitched the water out in the yard. I thought I'd better get to the front before they went back, and just made it in time.

This went on and on like this, and after three or four times I got tired of watching 'em. I kept telling myself it wasn't fair to Mom for Pap to be acting like this behind her back.

But I wasn't the kind of person to tell. I had to get somebody else to do it for me. For the past couple of months I had been trying to think of a way to let Mom know without Pap thinking I was the one who told her. And that day while I was up there getting that egg, it all came to me.

When I got back, I gave Miss Molly Bee the egg, and me and Pap told her good night and left for the quarters. We got home just before sundown. Mom cleaned the fishes and fried 'em, and we sat at the table, the three of us, and ate in silence. Nobody ever talked at Mom's table; she didn't go for that. I looked over at Mom. I loved her very much. I loved Pap, too. I loved both of 'em. And since I was their only little grandchild, I thought it was my duty to see that nothing ever separated 'em. Death, maybe, but that was all.

So the next day when I finished all my work, I went down the quarters and told Lucius what I wanted him to do.

"Listen, Lucius," I said. "This is what. You come up home 'round two o'clock. By then Mom ought to be through with her work and ought to be on the gallery cooling off. Somebody'll probably be out there with her—Aunt Lou, Miss Olive, or somebody. But you come up there 'round two. And we'll play little bit, and then sit on the steps. Now we'll wait till they're quiet. Remember, wait till they're quiet. Then I want you to say this, and I want you to say it plain. I want you to say, 'Didn't I see you and Pap going toward Miss Molly Bee yesterday?' That's all I want you to say. 'Didn't I see you and Pap going toward Miss Molly Bee yesterday?' I'll take it from there. Now, can you remember that, Lucius?"

"Uh-huh."

"Say it."

"Didn't I see y'all going—"

"I didn't say 'Y'all,' Lucius. I said, 'You and Pap.' Remember 'Pap.' You got to say 'Pap.' Now say it."

"Didn't I see you and Pap at Miss Molly Bee—"

"I didn't say 'at' neither, Lucius. I said, 'going.' 'Going' make her wonder little bit. Now say it."

"Didn't I see you and Pap going toward Miss Molly Bee yesterday?"

"That's right. Say it again."

Lucius said it again, and I made him say it about ten more times. After a while he had it down so pat and could say it so fast, even I couldn't keep up with him. So I slowed him up till he got it at just the right speed. I even told him how to hold his head and how to look at me when he was saying it. You had to really work with Lucius to make him get things the right way.

Sure enough, 'round two he came up there; and sure enough, Mom was sitting out on the gallery fanning and talking to Miss Olive Jarreau. Me and Lucius made a ring on the ground and shot marbles all the time Mom and Miss Olive was talking. Then when I seen the conversation began to slow up, I told Lucius let's sit on the steps. We sat there—I don't know how long—ten, fifteen minutes— and then I looked at Lucius. Old Lucius was waiting.

"Hey?" he said. "Didn't I see you and Pap going toward Miss Molly Bee yesterday?"

"Me and Pap?" I said.

Lucius looked at me, and didn't know what to say. We hadn't rehearsed nothing else, you see.

"Oh, yeah, it was you and Pap," he said. "You and Pap. You and Pap. Uh-huh. You and Pap."

"I doubt it," I said. "We went fishing yesterday. There ain't no fishing pond by Miss Molly Bee's house."

"I'm sure it was you and Pap," Lucius said. "You and Pap."

I looked at Lucius to make him shut up, 'cause I knowed Mom had heard and Miss Olive Jarreau had heard, too. It was quiet after that—what you call a dead silence. I had my back toward 'em, but I could feel Mom looking at me. Miss Olive was probably looking down the quarters, since that's the way her chair was faced. Then after a while I could feel Mom looking out at the tree in front of the house. And Miss Olive looked somewhere else, too. And then Mom looked at me again, 'cause I could feel her eyes on the back of my neck. And Miss Olive must have looked somewhere else, 'cause I could feel that, too. Then a little later she said she had to be going. And soon after she said it, Lucius said it, too. I reckoned Lucius thought I was going to get a whipping, and he didn't want to be anywhere 'round.

But nothing like that happened. Mom didn't even say a word. She just kept looking at me. I had my back toward her, but I could feel her eyes. You can feel it when people are looking at you. Especially old people.

Pap showed up not too long after Miss Olive and Lucius had gone home. He took a seat on the gallery and leaned back against the post.

"Ooooo, it's hot," he said.

"It sure is," Mom said, like nothing had happened.

"Think I'll go fishing tomorrow," Pap said. "Would have gone today, but it was too hot."

"They biting out in the river right smartly," Mom said.

"They biting better back in the field," Pap said.

"Talking to Aunt Lou this morning," Mom said. "Told me she caught a big mess few days back."

"They still biting better back in the field," Pap said. "Know a spot where they really biting back there."

"Well, go where you want," Mom said.

"They almost jumping out the bayou back in the field," Pap said.

Now I could feel that Mom was looking at Pap. Pap didn't know that Mom knowed, so he was looking over in the garden, probably thinking about Miss Molly Bee. And Mom, who knowed, probably also knowed what he was thinking about, and so she just sat there watching him.

"When you get through with your work, there, tomorrow," Pap said to me, "dig us up a good cup of worms."

"He can't go with you tomorrow," Mom said. "Want him to go somewhere with me."

"Yes?" Pap said. "Where at?"

"Ohhh, just somewhere," Mom said.

"Well," Pap said. "Guess I'll have to make it all by myself."

"Yes," Mom said. "You do that."

So the next day, right after dinner, Pap went out in back and dug him a cup of worms. He hollered in at us he was leaving, then I saw him going out the gate with that little bent fishing pole.

"Get your hat," Mom said.

I put on my hat and went on the gallery to wait for her. After she had closed up all the windows and doors, we left the house. At first we started out the same way Pap had gone, but after a little while we turned down another road. We walked and walked, neither one of us saying a word. If there's anything I'm not supposed to ask Mom, that's Where we going? If she wants me to know, she tells me. If she don't tell me, I'm supposed to wait and see.

So we walked and walked. Passing patches of cane after patches of cane. Then patches of corn, then patches of cotton. We went farther and farther back in the fields.

Then we came up to a house. I had heard plenty about this house, but I hadn't ever come there. Madame Toussaint, an old hoodoo lady, lived in it, and none of us children wouldn't go nowhere near it.

The house was old and leaning to one side, and the fence and the gate was all broken down. They had a big pecan tree right in front of the door, and the yard was covered with weeds.

I pulled the gate open for Mom, since she couldn't jump over it, and we went in the yard.

"Stay here," she told me.

I sat on the steps and Mom went up on the gallery and knocked three times. I heard a dog bark three times. He must been a big dog, 'cause I know he had a heavy voice. Then I heard Madame Toussaint ask who it is. Mom said it was her, and Madame Toussaint unlocked her door, and Mom went in.

I felt a little scary out there all by myself, 'cause I had heard the people say Madame Toussaint could do all kinds of strange things.

C. Hugh said one time he passed by here and one of Madame Toussaint's chickens spoke to him. The chicken said, "What you know, C. Hugh?" C. Hugh said he looked over his shoulder and there was nothing standing there but that chicken, grinning at him. C. Hugh said that's the last time he seen that chicken, the last time he seen that house, and the last time he ever passed by here day or night. C. Hugh said by the time he reached that road that took you to the quarters, he was running so fast, he ran over in Montemare cane field. Said he knocked down almost a whole row of cane 'fore he got on the road again. Said when he hit that road, he started praying. Said he said, "Lord, don't let me meet up with nothing, 'cause anything I meet up with go'n have to die. Mule, horse, cow, or tractor, I'm going over it." But said he didn't meet nothing, thank God, till he got home.

The dog barked again and made me jump. That dog had the loudest voice I ever heard on a dog. Then after he had barked, Mom came out and told me let's go. I was sure glad to get away from the place.

The next time Pap asked me to go fishing with him, Mom said I couldn't 'cause she had something for me to do. Pap said that was too bad, and he went outside and dug his worms and got his little bent pole and headed toward the back. I watched him go, and I felt a little sad. Eggs or no eggs, Miss Molly Bee or no Miss Molly Bee, I liked fishing with Pap.

After he had gone, Mom took me by the arm and led me on the gallery. She told me to sit on the steps and keep my eyes on that woodpecker in our mulberry tree. We had a mulberry tree right in the front yard, and, sure enough, there was a woodpecker up there pecking.

"What for?" I said. "I wish I had my slingshot. I'll keep my eyes on him. I'll—"

"Boy?" Mom said. She looked at me in that mean way she got of looking when she wants me to pay attention. She glanced at the woodpecker and looked at me again. "When he fly away, you count to thirty and let me know."

"Suppose he don't fly? I want to go shoot marbles."

"If he peck there all day, you stay there."

"Suppose he stay there all night?"

Mom looked at me again in that mean way.

"Yes, ma'am," I said.

"I hate what I'm doing," she said. "But I can't help it. Letting that yellow woman make a fool of him like that."

She went inside, and I sat on the steps watching that woodpecker. Then when I got tired sitting, I lay back and looked at him. Then when I got tired lying there, I sat up again. When Lucius came by and asked me to shoot marbles with him, I told him I had to watch that woodpecker. Lucius asked me what I had to watch a woodpecker for. I told him for Mom. Lucius didn't know what I was talking about, but he sat there and watched him with me. Then after a while, he got tired and left. That doggone woodpecker was still up there, pecking and pecking away. Once he stopped for about a second, then he started all over again.

Then 'round five-thirty he gave it up and flew over the house. I counted to thirty right fast and ran inside to tell Mom.

"Get your hat," she said. "Let's go down to Mr. Étienne."

We went down there, and Mr. Étienne was in the back just getting ready to unhitch his mules. Mom asked him could she borrow his wagon for a while, and Mr. Étienne looked at her kind of funny-like. But when Mom promised to take good care of the mules, he said all right.

She told me to get in the wagon and take the lines, and she went and opened the gate. When I drove out in the road, she made me turn right. She locked the gate and climbed in, and we headed into the field.

Mom didn't say another word to me. Every time I asked her which way, she pointed her finger. I'd pull the lines, and the mules would go in that direction. The mules were tired and didn't want to go at all, so every now and then I had to give 'em a little pop. Mom didn't say anything to me, but I could feel she wanted to.

We went on and on, and then I seen we was headed toward Miss Molly Bee's house. I looked at Mom 'cause I still didn't know what was going on. But she just sat there quietly and looked straight ahead.

When we came up to the gate that took you in the pasture, Mom stood up in the wagon and started looking 'round. She looked right, she looked left. Then as she was getting ready to look right again, she jerked her head back the other way.

"There he is over there," she said.

I stood up to look, and, sure enough, there was Pap lying over there all tangled up in the wire fence. Mom opened the gate, and I drove over where Pap was. Pap was mumbling something to himself, but he wasn't moving. Mom told me to get down and help her get him in the wagon. We had a hard time untangling Pap out of that barbwire, but we managed to get him free. Then we got him in, and I gathered up the line and the string of fishes and laid them beside him. Pap was mumbling so much, Mom had to sit in the bed of the wagon and hold him in her arms.

"It's all right," she kept whispering to Pap. "It's all right."

When we got home, the sun had gone down. I helped Mom get Pap inside, then I took the mules back to Mr. Étienne. When I got back home, Pap was really mumbling. Over and over—"Get him away from me. Get him away from me." Pap mumbled like that all night. "Get him away from me. Get him away from me."

When Pap was able to talk, about a week later, he told us what had happened. He really got excited when he told us about it. I had never seen Pap get so excited before.

"My way home from fishing—" he said.

"From where?" Mom cut him off.

"Fishing. My way home from fishing—"

"From where?" Mom said.

Pap started to say he was on his way home from fishing again, but he stopped and looked at Mom.

"You know?" he said.

"I know," Mom said.

Pap looked at her a good while, then he nodded his head.

"You right. I was on my way from her house. I was walking slowly, walking slowly. Then all a sudden I heard this cissing. Didn't know what it was at first. Never heard nothing like it before—hope to never hear nothing like it again. Looked over my shoulder, couldn't see a thing. Soon as I start walking, could hear it. Cissing, cissing. Coming from back in the woods. Look back; nothing. Go little farther, then it get closer, and I hear it plainer. Look back. They got a snake there ten foot long. Never seen one like that before. Crawling on just half his belly. Head part straight up in the air. Looking straight at me—just cissing. I start running. Thing cissing—coming after me. I stop. He stop. I start walking. He come little bit, too. I stop. Thing stop. I break at him. Thing break back. I stop. He stop. I look at him. He look at me. I move my head one way. He move his head. 'Lord have mercy,' I say. 'This the devil? This the devil?'

Thing just look at me, going 'Ciss-ciss.' I start walking. Here he come. I stop. He stop. I break at him and swing my pole at his head. Thing duck. I swing the other way. Thing duck again. Must hit fifty times at him, ain't hit him yet. 'This ain't no real snake,' I say. 'This ain't no real snake. This must be a haint.' And when I said that, I headed for home. Me, that haint, and that road. Faster I run, faster that haint run. Haint right behind me, going 'Ciss-ciss.' Getting close to the gate, haint get right side me, going 'Ciss-ciss.' Then I see that haint making me run 'cross the pasture—toward the fence. Come to the fence, didn't even think, just went in. Haint knowed what he was doing. Got me all tangled up and tried to beat me to death. Lord, have mercy. Lord, have mercy. You ain't been beaten by a haint, you ain't been beaten. When I woke up, I was home. Don't know nothing. Don't know nothing. Nothing but that haint."

Pap must have told that story about fifty times, and every time he told it he told it the same way, so it had to be the truth.

But that was a week later. The night we brought Pap home, Pap twisted and turned and mumbled all night. Mom sat up with him, bathing the cuts on his back and feeding him soup. I wanted to stay up with her, but she made me go to bed. When I woke up the next morning, there was Pap again—mumbling and groaning. People heard Pap was sick and they came by to see him. But Pap didn't recognize a soul, just sweating and mumbling. People told Mom she ought to get him a doctor, but Mom said Pap was her man, not theirs, and she knowed how to look after him. People wouldn't argue with Mom; nobody ever argued with Mom. But they kept on dropping by to look at Pap. Everybody dropped by. That is, everybody but Miss Molly Bee. She passed by the house couple times and peeped in, but that was all. One time I met her in the road and she asked me how was Pap feeling. I said he was doing pretty good. She smiled and told me to tell Pap she said hello. I told Pap. Pap didn't say a word. He just gazed at the ceiling. Then he started talking about the haint again. That haint just stayed in Pap's mind. Nothing else. Just the haint. And everything led up to the haint. If you said berry, Pap would put berry with bush, bush with pasture, and pasture with haint. If you said post, Pap would put post with fence, fence with pasture, and pasture with haint. If you said dirt, water, sky—anything; it all added up to haint.

But after about a week or so, Pap was able to get up. His legs were still wobbly, and he couldn't do much, but he could at least go out on the gallery and sit in the sun. And the first day Pap went out there, Pap surprised me. Because that was the first time I'd ever seen Pap sit in a chair on the gallery. He set right by the door across from Mom. And Mom was some proud of it. You could see it and you could feel it.

Not too long after we had been sitting out there, Lucius came by. Me and Lucius played marbles a few minutes, then we sat on the steps. I waited till Mom and Pap were quiet, then I looked at Lucius. Lucius said, "Passed by Miss Molly Bee's house yesterday, and Miss Molly Bee was laughing to kill Caesar."

I could tell Mom and Pap was looking at Lucius, and I said, "What was she laughing about?"

Lucius said, "Don't know. But she sure was laughing. Back there in her kitchen, laughing to beat the band."

A week after Pap was up, he was able to go fishing again. I dug a big cup of worms, and we left the house. Just as I was turning down the quarters, Pap stopped me.

"Where you going?" he said.

"Ain't we going fishing?"

"We going," he said.

"Well, ain't —?"

"That's the only fishing hole you know?" he said.

"You mean we going to the river?"

Pap didn't say anything, and started walking. I ran and caught up with him.

"Ehh, y'all sure think you smart, huh?" he said.

"Who, Pap?" I said.

"Madame Toussaint. Who else?" he said.

I didn't say anything. I liked old Pap. I liked Mom, too.

"What a haint," Pap said. "What a haint."

In His Own Words:
Ernest J. Gaines
—— *in Conversation* ——

A Literary Salon:
Oyster/Shrimp Po'boys,
Chardonnay, and Conversation
with Ernest J. Gaines

Ernest J. Gaines, Marcia Gaudet, and Darrell Bourque
December 17, 2002

DB: That whole idea of influence or use or whatever you want to call it is really broad. I mean to a large extent any of us who are writers or musicians or visual artists are all influenced by the larger culture that we encounter. But what we could do in this particular set of interviews is to ask some more specific questions about how artistic expression impacts a particular imagination. As we've talked to you over the years informally and in other essays or interviews that you've given, you know, there are instances where you talk about the way in which you listened to Joyce, read Joyce, read Turgenev, loved the work of Vincent van Gogh, and so forth. And so in a lot of ways, I think that one of the reasons why your name immediately came up for me is because I know that as you've talked through the years, you've touched on some of those ideas. But I was wondering, Ernie, who would you say is a nonliterary artist who has maybe had an impact on you as a writer or as an artist yourself? Are there any people who come to mind?

GAINES: A nonliterary artist?

DB: Right, either a musician or—

GAINES: Well, I've listened to music all my life, all my adult life I should say, and especially the classical music, symphonies as well as chamber music. I like to listen to jazz music, a lot of jazz music, of course. And a lot of blues, a lot of spirituals. Pop music. And I think without knowing how directly it's influenced me, I think it has influenced me. I think I've taken from so many different artists that it's hard for me to pinpoint it to one particular musician. Although I've listened to pieces of music, like the *New World Symphony* of Dvořák. And because of the motifs or themes of spirituals and themes in the symphony, it's awakened something in me when I've listened to it.

MG: I want to go back to what you said sixteen years ago. You said at that time that music helped you develop as a writer, and while writing *Miss Jane Pittman*, you played Mussorgsky's *Pictures at an Exhibition*. You also said that some of the best descriptions of things, especially dealing with blacks, have been described better in music, especially the great blues singers like Bessie Smith, Josh White, and Leadbelly. And also in jazz music—a repetition of things, understatement, playing around the note.

GAINES: Right, right. Yes, I agree. Bessie Smith's "Backwater Blues," and I feel that I get the sensation, the description, and the feeling of it—of the Flood of '27, as I get when I read Faulkner's "Old Man." That sharp picture that she gives in two and a half lines of singing, I get a picture of what it must have been like—for the people—the water, and life at that particular time. Leadbelly singing about the prisons—at Angola or the prisons in Texas. I get a good feeling of what prison life was like. Regarding that influence in some of my work—Lightnin' Hopkins singing "Mr. Tim Moore's Farm"—I think that influenced me in writing some of the books. When I wrote *Of Love and Dust*, a man was put on the farm to work his time out. That had an influence on me. And I listened to the spirituals, and I used that kind of, those kinds of emotions when writing scenes of older women—for example, in *A Gathering of Old Men* or in *A Lesson Before Dying*—how they talked to God, and the associations about God. I think that's from listening to that.

MG: Do you think the contemporary singers—and I have in mind especially B. B. King, because I think you said you liked B. B. King. I'm not talking about rap music—

GAINES: I don't know a thing about rap—

MG: Artists like B. B. King—do you get that same kind of feeling or influence?

GAINES: I do. I think I do. I think the *early* B. B. King. The B. B. King of the fifties. You see, I've been listening to B. B. King since the fifties. Definitely. I have those records. And it's not as sophisticated as it is today. There's a young musician—who's compared to B. B. King—called Robert Cray. And he's just a fantastic blues singer. And he sings contemporary things. The way he sings about these contemporary problems—I went through those problems as a young man in the forties. And he's young. I guess in his forties—youn compared to B. B. King. So I'm still very much influenced by th blues singers. Especially the rural singers, much more than the url blues singers.

MG: I wonder about the influence of rap. The rap singers much a part of the mainstream culture right now—and not o influence on young African-American culture. But it seem *urban* thing, and so removed from the experiences of the older generations.

GAINES: Right. I don't understand a thing about it. I don't understand it at all. I can't even talk about it.

DB: I think one of the interesting things about rap music is the way in which it cuts across a racial divide, so that young white kids are as interested in black rap music as young black kids. And it goes both ways. Some of Eminem's strongest and most fervent fans are young black kids. And it's just a phenomenon to me that I don't understand, either, but there's a kind of ability to communicate and something going on there that I think is not for our generation.

MG: But in a way the blues and jazz singers did the same thing.

DB: Yeah. That's interesting. I hadn't thought about that.

MG: It just may be the form that generation needed. And that was my other question, do you think that the great blues and jazz singers did serve that purpose—of sort of appealing very widely? They were singing often about specific black experiences, but they reached a larger audience.

GAINES: Yes, I think that definitely happened. And I don't know where Elvis Presley would be today if it were not for black musicians. And the group that really made white America aware of the influence of blues—especially rural blues—was the Rolling Stones from England. They were the first white group to really come out and say, "Yes, definitely, we've been influenced by these people." By Muddy Waters, and Chuck Berry, and all of these black singers. These blues singers definitely influenced many of the white singers. This young man who died in a plane crash several years ago—from Texas—Stevie Ray Vaughan—a tremendous blues musician, and you can see the influence of black music on him. So it's definitely there. Go back to jazz, as you said, Benny Goodman with the Count Basie Band, how they integrated, how they worked together and made good music. Benny Goodman had people like Charlie Christian on guitar, and Lionel Hampton on the xylophone. Teddy Wilson on the piano. So it's always been out there. I can understand that. That stuff that's called "hip-hop"—I can't understand. I don't know what they're doing. I was at a place recently, at one of these readings, and one guy got up and asked me, "Mr. Gaines, what do you think of hip-hop music, as a writer?" What's hip-hop? I had no idea what they were talking about.

MG: And what's almost frightening to me is that I can remember—not so much with my dad because he was a musician, and he loved blues and jazz—but with Chuck Berry and others and when rock and roll became mainstream—and now my generation is questioning whether rap, or hip-hop, really is an art form.

GAINES: I think of contemporary jazz—and when they came out with bebop—you know, nobody wanted to accept it. You know, the old traditionalists didn't want to accept bebop. But then the artists and industry and all those guys stuck to it—

DB: And now we can hear it. You couldn't even hear it early on. Your ears wouldn't accept it—

GAINES: Right—but it's out there. John Coltrane, when he changed music around, people didn't understand what he was doing. But John Coltrane was a genius. That was another influence on my work—listening to it—because it's really rooted in the blues. If you really listen to John Coltrane, it's really blues all the time—blues and spirituals all the time.

DB: You were mentioning Elvis Presley a while ago, and a little fact about Elvis Presley is his love of gospel music. He would come off the stage after a performance at midnight, and at five or six in the morning, his singers, his backup singers were still backstage. He would make them sing gospel music, and he would just go on until daybreak. And it wasn't something that happened at a stage in his career. It was all the way through. And I think that he drew to a large extent from the same thing—from the blues and the spirituals.

GAINES: Yes, sure.

MG: And he didn't see that as a sort of a divide. And I wonder about that—the idea that there is sort of a break between the spirituals and blues or jazz—and even that expression, that one is much more "God's music" and the other is sort of like "the Devil's music."

GAINES: I think the artist must deal with both God and the Devil. I think you can't put one aside or the other. You know, like if you're going to write for certain groups, and I don't believe in writing for any specific group. So let others call blues the "sin music" and gospel is God's music, just as the minister does in *A Lesson Before Dying*. You know, when they visit Jefferson in jail, and he's playing that radio and he's listening to blues, the old man—the minister—says "that sin box." Well, sometimes that sin box can help you get to heaven as well as anything else. That's what I was trying to show. But the artist himself cannot separate the religious or the blues or the spiritual. The artist cannot.

MG: Yes, I think that was always an outside judgment, because the artists saw that some of their inspiration for the blues and jazz came from the deeply spiritual.

GAINES: Yes, he must—he has to use both of them.

DB: The minister—and that's so beautifully drawn in your various works—has a narrower mission.

GAINES: Right. He's there to save the soul, but what about the everyday life? And that's what the artist must deal with. He must deal not only with the soul but with both. That's Grant and the minister's argument. It's Reverend Moses' argument—just as the nihilist and the minister in "The Sky Is Gray."

MG: What you're saying reminds me of the ideas about the nature of religion and the sacred and profane—Émile Durkheim's concept of sacred and profane and Mircea Eliade's *The Sacred and the Profane*. It's all part of life, and you can't completely separate it.

DB: And if you start thinking that there is a separation, then you've in some way desecrated the sacred, and elevated the profane in a way. This may be a silly question, Ernie, but I've often wondered if I were a filmmaker—I remember that scene in the café in "The Sky Is Gray" where the man asks the woman to get up to dance and so forth, and when they make the film, of course, the filmmaker has to put a song in there for them to dance to. And this is just speculation, and as I said, this may be silly, but if you were consulted by the filmmaker, what are some of the possible songs that you would have had them have on the jukebox? Because I think that's an important way that you—

GAINES: Oh, I don't know now if I could just come up with any song. I'm sure if I would think about it for a while, about jazz and stuff, I would come up with the right song, but I can't think of any specific song. I know it should be a sort of slow beat, but I couldn't think of a particular title. You know what happened about this particular scene? The tune that this guy played on that record was written by a friend of the director. That's the music played in the film. It was not a tune that was a traditional one that I knew about, or anyone else knew about. But it was written for this specific film.

MG: One of the things I wanted to ask you about—and again this is in relation to the idea of how art forms express things about life that we perhaps don't see in other media. And again I'm quoting you, and this was in John Lowe's book *Conversations with Ernest Gaines*. In one of the interviews there, you said, ". . . we all are naïve about the true history of blacks in this country. We have DuBois, Douglass, and Booker T. Washington, but we don't have the story of the average black who has lived to be that age." How does *art* (as opposed to straight history) broaden that perspective? How does art, literature, music sort of fill in that story? Do you see art or literature or music as giving us that history that the written historical record doesn't include?

GAINES: I think so, because you get so much more of the experience of the everyday man, of the common man, in music—especially music, and music is so much out there that you can hear music all the time. You can hear music on the radio, on recordings, so it's always there for you. And it tells you much more about yourself than history books because so many people were not able to read the history books. And music just filled in for them. Literature, I think, was the same thing for those who had the chance, who were able to read. I think now all across the country, in eight or nine different cities, people are discussing *A Lesson Before Dying.* And wherever I go I find people, most often white people, saying, "I did not know this" or "I did not know that, and this changes my life." Someone told me about a year ago, at graduation night, "I just read your book *A Lesson Before Dying*, and it changed my life." Someone told me the same thing in Richmond, Virginia. "It changed my life." Just writing about the everyday people, and literature does that, or literature can do that. A person like Jefferson or a person like Tante Lou or a person like Miss Emma—those people are never written about in a history book. And quite often are never written about in a newspaper, and so literature can bring that to life.

MG: In some ways, that sort of unwritten history, or unwritten in the history book, that sort of thing would have been in oral tradition. In some ways, we always had the stories in the culture about people like Tante Lou or people like Jefferson, but that often didn't leave that community. That was very local. So it was not known to those people who did not have access to the story in oral tradition. In some ways, the writer gives those stories access to a wider audience (or a wider audience access to those stories), so the writer is more important to the outsider than to the person in the community who at least might have gotten a version of those, who knew more about these. Do you think that's still true for the younger generation? Do they get those things through oral tradition?

GAINES: I don't—maybe they get it through that rap. Maybe that's what they're talking about. Maybe—I almost feel that that's what they're talking about. They're communicating something out there for people to be so much impressed by it. As you said, the white kids are doing it. You go to France, you find French kids are doing it. I'm pretty sure they're doing the same thing in Japan. So, it is going on. It's something that I cannot understand, but they wouldn't understand—well, I can't say they don't understand me, now, because the book is being read from the middle years in school to the university level, and I'm constantly getting letters from the students—teachers make them write the letters—but letters from the students about the book.

DB: I think one of the things that great art always has the potential to do is sort of crack us open in a way—to crack us open and to show us something that we didn't know before, and I think that person at the graduation or that woman in Richmond, you know, were saying that. Because I think we live in a time where we're not aware that we're living in a time where there's a great need for spiritual rooted-ness, and I think when they pick up the book and read *A Lesson Before Dying* or "The Sky Is Gray," or one of your other stories, that's one of the things that it puts them in touch with—that spiritual rootedness, or being rooted in something that is sacred. And I think one of the things that your works do so well is to show that there is a sacredness in the everyday life.

MG: We haven't touched upon the influence of visual art.

DB: And you're a photographer.

MG: Yes, and we've talked about how music has influenced you. But what about the visual arts? I know that you're a really great photographer, and the photographs you took, especially at River Lake Plantation, serve as documents in a way. How do you think art, paintings, and pictures, and photographs, both by other artists and the things you've done—how do you see that and what does that bring to your whole idea of art?

GAINES: Well, the photographs remind me of a time, remind me of a place, and of a people, that I write about. Without those photographs, I don't know that I could recall as accurately the things that I'd like to write about. And seeing the paintings by someone like Van Gogh. I'm thinking about *The Potato Eaters* now. People sitting around the table. That awakened something in my mind, and I can recall that I did the same thing. There's a lamp on the table, people sitting at the table, blessing the food, eating, and the place. That brings it back to my memory—to what I saw as a child. A workman's shoes, those all-muddy shoes, you know, brogans, that snaps my mind back to the past where we wore those same kind of shoes, and I've seen the people kick them off their feet and leave them out on the porch or something like that. Those kind of things that just remind me of my own past, so I can draw from that.

MG: You've talked about *Vincent's Room*, and how that sort of gave you an image of the order, of arrangements—

GAINES: Yes, I have a picture of *Vincent's Room* in my study out there. Yes, of the minimum of things you actually need—you can get by with so little. And I try to do that with my work. You don't have to overblow things. I mean, I'm incapable of writing using a broad stroke. I have to use a smaller pen, be very selective. I think I prefer to repeat something three times to get it over, than to use a broad pen to get it over.

DB: I'm reading a book right now on Vincent van Gogh, and what you're saying reminds me of something he's saying in that book. He says that he doesn't—he can admire the beautifully finished and the well-finished painting of the seventeenth century, but what he loves about Rembrandt is that there are parts of it that are unfinished. There are parts of it where you see the brush of the real man in there. And that strikes me as sort of close to what you're saying about your stories. That they're about the little things, about the brogan that can bring you to a particular memory, or about the potato eaters. And it occurred to me, too, that as you were describing *The Potato Eaters*, when he talks about that painting, he says— you were talking about blessing the food, eating the food and blessing the food—and he says that one of the influences for that painting was Christ at Emmaus, where Christ has to deal with a few of his followers after the Crucifixion and before he is actually ascended. So he sees that as a sacred painting, and I thought that was interesting that in what you said, up to this point, about the job of the artist to marry the sacred and the everyday, the sacred and the ordinary.

MG: You mentioned the lamp, and I'm sort of fascinated with—we called them coal oil lamps—

GAINES: Right, coal oil lamps.

MG: And it's almost a nostalgic thing I have about coal oil lamps. My dad used to sell coal oil in his drugstore. When you have a drugstore in a rural area you sell lots of different things. And one of the big things that people would come to get every day was coal oil to fill the lamps. The coal oil lamps—was that something you had in your home when you were growing up?

GAINES: Definitely so. I learned to read with a coal oil lamp. You see, we had no electricity on the plantation until after the war, so that was about '45 or '46, about two years before I left. But for my first twelve years, I'm pretty sure, there was no electricity, so we read by the lamp on the table or the fire in the fireplace.

MG: You know, I was thinking, too, when you were talking about the lamp on the table, and often the coal oil lamp was on the table.

GAINES: Right. It was set on the mantel until you had to read or to study, and then you read like that. But when you were there just for illuminating the room, it was on the mantel. The clock would be there, too.

MG: Maybe I'm romanticizing this too much, and I'm thinking of *The Potato Eaters*, where you saw the images, you saw the objects that the light touched, and you didn't see the whole picture.

GAINES: Right, the place was transformed by that light. These are the kinds of things that I find in the movies as well—and I see what the camera can do. I've been influenced by all of these things. Not one thing or two things, but all of these things. I remember I used to do a lot of walking in San Francisco in the morning, and there was this old man who used to sweep the streets before we got the motorized street sweepers in San Francisco. He used to sweep the streets, and whenever I'd come back from my walk in the park, I'd see him pushing his broom. And, you know, I'd talk about baseball or football or whatever. But he would never leave a piece of paper or a piece of anything without brushing it up and moving it along to pick it up. And I thought, it's a wonderful thing that this man, this street sweeper, that he's so particular about everything that he does. That little piece of trash—to be sure that it's done. I feel the same way with my writing. The little things—you be sure that they're corrected. Don't leave it there if it's not necessary. So I learned—you asked if I learned from the visual arts and from music—but I also learned from watching the everyday person, what he does, how he does something. Or watch a great athlete—see how they place themselves, how they do things so smoothly. So writing, for me, is not just learning from novelists or short-story writers, but from all the things around us.

DB: Talking about visuals, it seems to me—and I don't mean in any way to make a statement about your story—but it seems to me in so many of your stories, you get the story right out there right away. You know, like the basic parts of the story—in *A Lesson Before Dying*, right away we know what happened. And it seems like so much of the rest of your story is about drawing characters.

GAINES: Yes, right, that's what it is about. Yes, in the beginning, in the first chapter, you know what has happened, and the people that are going to be involved, but the rest of it is, ah—I said one time—

Oprah asked me who I was trying to reach, and I said I tried to create characters with character to improve my own character and the character of that person who might read it. So it is what happens to the characters after this tragedy has happened. And the rest of it is—portraits.

DB: When we were talking about visual art, I couldn't help noting that one of the things you use to make a story is drawing these portraits. In that book I'm reading about Van Gogh, he said that was the thing. He said, "Portraits—that's what I want to do, portraits." And it reminds me of you because that's what you do. In *A Lesson Before Dying*, you know, from the beginning to the end with Miss Emma, for instance, you don't have the complete portrait until the end of the book, and there's the drawing of that portrait, the drawing of Jefferson's portrait, and it's just this beautiful collection of portraits. And I felt the same way about *A Gathering of Old Men*.

GAINES: Yes, yes. I know when I was writing *The Autobiography of Miss Jane Pittman*, I was thinking about titling it *Sketches of a Plantation*. I think what I'm possibly doing is sketching and writing letters. Writing letters is like sketching.

DB: Yes, and you know I feel that those kinds of group portraits that Rembrandt was so famous for. I know that you're working in a completely different place and you have a different objective, but to me, *A Gathering of Old Men* is a beautiful collection of group portraits. I don't know who did the cover art, the dust jacket, but it seems to me that they had the idea in mind—of that old seventeenth-century Dutch masters group portrait.

GAINES: Right, yes.

DB: Can you talk a little bit more about—I remember you told us one time about listening to classical music and you talked about the music, the Mussorgsky, that you were listening to when you were writing *Miss Jane Pittman*.

GAINES: Right, *Miss Jane Pittman*. I was writing about Miss Jane, and I was listening to *Pictures at an Exhibition*. The structure or frame is of this guy at an exhibition, and he was observing these pictures. And the motif would be as he moved from one picture to another, there was a motif and repetitive theme. At that particular time I was thinking about writing *Miss Jane* from the single point of view. It wasn't really *Miss Jane Pittman* yet. It was just *Sketches of a Plantation*. That was the original idea. But in order to have a common theme to connect those sketches, well, there would be this little old lady. Just sketches and sketches, and after each book, there would be this huge ending. There are four books—the War Years, Reconstruction, The Plantation, and The Quarters. And each one almost ends up in violence. And if you listen to the sketches in *Pictures at an Exhibition*, all of these characters are going through this piece of music. And at the very end, it's loud, loud Russian crazy music. "At Hell's Gate," I think it's called. But then I realized that music could only take me so far, and then without anything else, it wasn't going to work. With music, you can learn so much from it, but you could not repeat it in literature exactly as it was there. So I went over it, the sketches of the plantation that I did, the short biography of Miss Jane Pittman that I did, and I realized that I still was not getting the real character that I had to get. So I had to put all of that aside, and go back and do *Miss Jane Pittman*. But I started off with that *Pictures at an Exhibition* as the first influence on what I wanted to write about.

DB: I remember, Ernie, that one of the great thrills that I had in listening to *Pictures at an Exhibition* after you talked about what you had done and what your experiences with it had been and everything was to hear the *walking* music in *Pictures at an Exhibition*, and to realize how much walking that little woman did. Because she walks, yes, and that was so exhilarating for me to realize that.

GAINES: Well, I got that from—that walking stuff—so much I got from Eudora Welty's "A Worn Path." The walking and walking and walking. And that was also a good influence on "The Sky Is Gray." The walking and walking and going back and forth.

MG: You both have commented that blues was a good influence on the form you put "The Sky Is Gray" in.

GAINES: Oh, yes. "The Sky Is Gray" as well as *Of Love and Dust*. Especially *Of Love and Dust*, the blues form that's used in Lightnin' Hopkins there. And just one verse from Lightnin' Hopkins:

> *The worse thing this black man ever done*
> *Was move his wife and family to Mr. Tim Moore's farm.*
> *Mr. Tim Moore's man never stands and grin.*
>   *[That's the overseer.]*
> *He said, "You stay out the graveyard, nigger,*
>   *I'll keep you out the pen."*

And so I took that and dealt with Marcus. He would not go to the graveyard. I mean he would not be killed, and this guy here would keep him out of the pen. And the next verse was like:

> *But he wake you up so early in the morning.*
> *You catch a mule by his hind leg [to go to work].*

So those two verses were really what pushed the story. And, of course, I knew all the things I could bring in because I had lived on a plantation and I had seen things that happened around me, so I could bring other things into the story—government affairs, and all that stuff.

MG: I remember you saying that in "The Sky Is Gray" that indirection, "playing around the note," was an influence from the blues.

GAINES: Yes, I said it all the time. You don't have to see them thrown out of a store or a place where they're going to get something to eat uptown. You don't have to have that happen in order to get the feeling that this was a segregated world. Some things you don't have to come to directly and scream at. You just play it smoothly and that is even more painful for you, a reader, to see—this mother and child walking down this cold street without being able to go in to get warm or to get something to eat. It's so much more effective so that you leave some stuff out. But what you do is get that little line that really shows it exactly—that shows enough—and you leave the other stuff out. At least I feel that way.

MG: Yes. So it's sort of like in blues, you hear the melody and they always come back to it, but they're also going around it. We're seeing all the things related.

GAINES: Yes, right. I was listening to a great solo by Lester Young— playing "My Funny Valentine." And you very seldom hear "My Funny Valentine," but he's playing so much around it that you get a greater feeling for "My Funny Valentine" without really having to sing it. It's things like that I try to do when I'm writing.

DB: It seems that you also use the repetition as a formal device as well with that tooth and the mother and the son. They go in and they're pushed back out. They go in and they're pushed back out.

GAINES: Just like in *A Lesson Before Dying*. You don't have to see a guy going to the electric chair. You never see them pulling the thing and all that. That's been done before. You don't have to see it. You know, what I try to do is show the horror of it. Plus the exact way in which they brought the chair in and adjusted the thing, so they had the right corner, the wires in the right place, right near a window but pushed back into a corner, and all these little small details in the preparation to execute somebody. All these little things. To hear the generator from a long distance away. What I think is the most horrible thing is if you're standing up there. And as Paul says, he dropped his head, he lowered his head because he didn't want to look directly at the thing, but he heard the noise, and that's much more powerful. That's what I try to capture.

MG: One of the interesting things about having that kind of thing, like a generator—that struck me, in fact, when we saw the play this fall, is that idea of the "electric chair." The electric chair is so foreign to contemporary students, but then in talking about that, they were asking why there was a generator. Well, I'm not exactly sure, but it occurred to me that electricity was not yet the norm at that time and place. Those were sounds, like the sound of the generator, that were just totally foreign, that they would not have heard anywhere. And the idea of using this as a way of execution when electricity was not yet understood. It was not a part of the average home yet in rural Louisiana. And I think it struck me that the effect on the people witnessing it at that time was probably much greater than looking at it in terms of electricity, which is something taken for granted now. But both the sound [of the generator] and the idea of electricity were not the norm then—and then the *mis*use of it. Something that could be used for good but wasn't really available yet, and then a tremendous misuse of it.

GAINES: Another situation of getting around the whole thing instead of coming directly on it is the seductive scene between Marcus and Louise in the first scene in *Of Love and Dust*. Marcus is trying to break into the house where they are, and all you can hear is the noise in there and the running around the room in there. That, to me, is stronger than you seeing the physical thing going on. Just hearing this noise through that door, and then the silence. You don't hear any noise anymore and you know they're in there. You know, just playing around it.

MG: I think that playing around the note and the indirection you do so beautifully—and I know you're probably not interested in what the critics are saying—but one of the big things in linguistic anthropology now is the idea of *reported speech,* and what happens when the speech is reported by someone else. And I thought how much your novels use that—especially in *Of Love and Dust* but in *A Gathering of Old Men* and *A Lesson Before Dying* as well. And you've said that—that it's not that Grant has experienced it directly, but he reports what is told to him by someone else. I think someone needs to do an article on reported speech in Ernest Gaines's novels.

DB: I was reminded just a while ago when you were talking about Marcus and how a character gets created, and you talked one time about the relationship between Marcus and another important popular cultural figure, Muhammad Ali. Could you say a little bit about that?

GAINES: Well, when I wrote that book, I wanted for Marcus to be sort of with the "gab" of Muhammad Ali, and at the same time I wanted him to be somewhat like a guy I actually knew. And this guy lived in Baton Rouge, one of these Creole guys. And he was tough; this guy really was tough. And he was the kind of guy who could walk into a bar and say, "I can whip any man in the bar." And he got into a fight in Baton Rouge, and two guys jumped him, and he got his knife out, and he killed one of the guys. He killed one of the guys. And was sent up for seven years in Angola, but he got out in five. And his boss tried to keep him out—they thought he was defending himself, you know. And he had a chance to stay out, but he would not. He refused to stay. He said I'm going to pay my dues because I don't want to owe anything. So he went to Angola for five years, and he came back out. And they ran him out of Baton Rouge, ran him out of town, and so he went to Houston, Texas. But the word had gotten to Houston about this guy, and he picked up a woman in Houston, and they went to San Francisco. I had known him here in Louisiana, and I used to hang around with him in San Francisco. He'd walk into a bar and say, "I'll whip any man in the bar. Anybody want to fight me?" And I'd say, "Lionel, don't start that." And he'd say, "You scared." And I'd say, "Yes, you damn right. Somebody's going to challenge you, man." So, eventually, he would be killed—someone killed him. As a matter of fact, that happened the same weekend I came down here to start filming *The Autobiography of Miss Jane Pittman*. I had seen him a couple of days before I came down here, and he said, "Boy, I sure would like to be in that picture show. I'd sure like to be in the picture show. You think you could get me a little part in it?" I said, "I don't know." So he said, "I want to get on down there. Let's me and you get on down—drive down there." He was one of these guys working as a mechanic, and he had a bunch of old cars around the place—all together probably couldn't make one good car. But he wanted to get in one of those old Cadillacs and drive on down. I said, "I'm not going down there like that—probably couldn't get out of San Francisco." And so I left. I got a flight out, I think, on Thursday. And Saturday, a friend of mine came by to tell me that he had been killed. Anyway, Marcus was sort of based on him, but I wanted Muhammad Ali's gift (or ability) to talk, talk, talk. I was writing *Of Love and Dust* at the same time

Muhammad Ali was a young guy. I think he had just changed his name to Muhammad Ali in the mid-sixties. That would be '66 or '67. So that was based around him. His looks and everything about him—and Lionel had his color and so on, kind of lightish brown. And his looks and his clothes. So, those two guys I had in mind.

MG: And Muhammad Ali had that wonderful artistic ability with words. He could have been a poet.

GAINES: He was a poet; he was a poet and he was a great fighter, too. And Marcus, too, would fight anybody, day or night. And Lionel was the same.

MG: Was Proctor [in "Three Men"] based on him as well?

GAINES: Well, Proctor not as much. But it's the same sort of story. Proctor, you know, he decides he's going to go up, but Marcus is the sort who says "I'm not going to Angola. I'm getting out of that place." This is the same sort of story. Because I had written "Three Men" and offered it for publication in the collection of stories, but Bill Decker, my editor, said, "First, give me a novel." So, I said, okay, suppose someone like Proctor would try to get out of what happened? So in the novel, I changed the thing around.

DB: I did think a moment ago when you said that about Muhammad Ali being a poet, that you could make a case that Muhammad Ali taught the rappers how to rap.

MG: Yes, because he was the first to put what was always a part of the culture, especially playing the dozens and the rapping, out into the mainstream. And both because he was already a fighter and he already had the status of a champion, he made it much more acceptable. And then the black comedians took it over. Somebody eventually will do a study tracing how we got to rap. But I think you're right. Ali did have a great influence.

GAINES: Yes, and there's a group called the Last Poets, and they work that kind of music, too. And of course many, many years ago you had the groups (they didn't call them rap) . . . it was a long way in coming, signifyin' and all that.

DB: While we're talking about poetry, you know that a remarkable piece of literature to me is Jefferson's Notebook [from *A Lesson Before Dying*], and I think it's one of the great American poems in the last half of the twentieth century. And I just wondered if you could tell us a little bit about how you came to that piece—or what you wanted to do with that piece of writing. Because I think it's in some ways—probably not for you, but for us—in some ways it seems like such a brave piece of writing. Because all of a sudden the story is being told by people who have different kinds of effectiveness and facility with language. And then there's this thing that comes up in the book that's disarming because it's so pure, and it's so beautiful. And I wonder what you were trying to do—if you could talk a little bit about that.

GAINES: I was trying to have this person, this human person, who, ah—within a few weeks of his death—does this thing where he identifies himself as a human being on trial. Everything is "trying" for Jefferson. He tries to say something about himself as a human being. What does he believe in? What does he think? We don't know him, I think, until he starts his diary. We don't know a man until he speaks. He's trying to say something, to show who he is. We have these pictures of him provided by Grant, but we don't know what's inside of him. And that's what I needed to do. And I didn't want any kind of soliloquy or aria to stop the walk, and when they ask if he had any final words I didn't want for him to want to talk for an hour. I told my students I had no idea how I would solve this problem when I started to write the book. I had no idea there would be a diary. I had no idea there would be a radio in that story. I've used the analogy many times of getting on the train in San Francisco and going to New York. And you only know so much. You don't know everything. And the radio is one of the things that came up for me on the train trip, and the diary came up for me on that trip. I spent half of every year over the next seven working on the book—'85 to '92. So during those seven years, the idea of the radio and the notebook came up. I suppose if I had written the novel in three years, this wouldn't have happened. I don't know what would have happened. I have no idea. But for seven years I got to stand back and think. And, during the fall, I was teaching, and thinking all the time. And then I'd go back to San Francisco and write on that book. And, of course, I came up with the idea of the notebook. But the exact date I came up with it, I don't know. I knew I had to have him say something about his life—about what he believed in, about justice, and about God, and injustice, and everyday, routine stuff, you know. What is life about to him? What is meaningful to him? But he had to give us those things himself because he would not reveal them to Grant or to Miss Emma or to anyone else. He had to give it himself. And he writes it at night, when nobody is there. He scratches all over this—writes it so awkward—over the line, under the line, above the line, across the line—he's writing it without punctuation or capitalization or anything. He's just writing it down, trying to say something about his life.

DB: I remember right at the beginning—you know, Grant's been telling us about him all along—and I imagine him writing and not even being really aware of what's he's doing in the notebook except trying to express himself. But when he talks about telling Mr. Wiggins that the bluebird is singing—that's such a jolting thing, you know, because you think that you've never been brought there. And this guy is about to die, and he knows that's an inevitable thing, and he's hearing birds singing and imagining that they're blue. That's just incredible to hear.

MG: While Darrell was talking about the diary, I got out this other quote from *Porch Talk* where you said:

> I think art is order. I think art must be order, no matter what you do with it. I don't care what Picasso did with twisted faces and bodies—all that sort of thing—I think there has to be a form of order there, or it's not art. The novel to me is art. The short story is art. And there must be order. I don't care what the chaos is. You must put it in some kind of decent form.

And then you go on to say that to you that's sort of imposing that order on what may seem chaotic. And I think—

GAINES: I said that? That's pretty good. I don't know if I can say something good as that now.

MG: Yes, isn't that cool—and you said a few good things today, too. And it reminded me of this when we were talking earlier with Darrell about the diary—because you're taking something out of its normal form of written communication, and it at first appears to be chaos—and then you put this order on it, and it just becomes absolutely poetic. And I agree with Darrell. I think it is a form of poetry.

GAINES: Right, yes.

DB: You know that kind of slow revelation inside the notebook where he says that he's sorry for having said what he said about Vivian. And then at the end of the story when he goes back to being aware of the outside world again and what's going on outside of his cell, there's that beautiful kind of repetition that brings it all full circle. And the pieces for me are so beautifully constructed. I think that part of the thing that affects me so much about it as a kind of poem is the way in which the speaker is so unaware in a way of what's being said, but there's a complete human being there.

GAINES: Yes.

MG: Did you have a sense of—I would think maybe the dates—but did you have any other sense of how you were imposing that order on the diary other than dates?

GAINES: Well, I thought the diary had to elevate the story. I thought that was the point of elevation. I think the story could not just go— it could not just go as Grant telling it. It had to be—what is that thing Joyce called it—the epiphany, the thing that brings everything to light. It's the thing that raises it. It's the thing that—often someone says, "I enjoyed your book." But after you read the diary, if that does not elevate you, then I don't know what else to do.

MG: That's an interesting point, because we think of one of the functions of art is that it gives that uplifting—that there is a sense of being enlightened or braced up. And there is that response to the diary.

GAINES: That's what I wanted the diary to be—that uplift. He's talking about dying, and "I'm gonna die," and says the bluebird is singing, and he pauses for a while, and says I hear my teeth hitting, and I hear my heart, but I'm strong. I'm going to be brave. All these things are the uplifting in his mind. He's not going to be this coward they'll have to drag. He's not going to eat a whole gallon of ice cream with a pot spoon. He's going to eat a little Dixie cup of ice cream. All of these little things elevate him—to salvation, to the uplifting of the soul.

MG: I understand from my students and most other people who have talked about it, that few people can get through that diary without tears, but by the end of it, they're uplifted. By having gone through it, they survive it.

GAINES: Right, yes. Once you go through it, you feel better.

DB: And that part of the novel serves in the same way or it serves the same purpose—or has the same effect as the spiritual, too, because so often the spiritual is about something that's heavy and burdensome, and then finally we sing it because we know it's going to lift us.

MG: And even if we have tears while we're singing it, we know it's going to lead to uplifting.

GAINES: Right.

DB: I have just one more question, but while I was thinking of my last question, you mentioned Joyce's epiphany, and I know Joyce is an important figure for you and an important storyteller, and I wondered if you could say a little bit, maybe one or two things, that you learned from Joyce.

GAINES: The number-one thing that I suppose we all—modern and contemporary writers—learned from Joyce is the stream of consciousness. I learned from Joyce and Faulkner how to center your work on an area. And then the one-day thing I got from Joyce's

Ulysses. You can do almost anything you want in that one day. Joyce must have gotten it from Greek tragedy, but I definitely got it from Joyce. And I was trying to do it with "A Long Day in November," and I was trying to do it in *A Gathering of Old Men.* And in "The Sky Is Gray," how to put the story together. You know, in "The Sky Is Gray," I could have stretched out the story for weeks and months, and in *A Gathering of Old Men,* I could have stretched on for months. So that, and the concentration of your work in one locale—all came from Joyce . . . and Faulkner.

DB: In a lot of ways when I look at your work and I try to see what literary traditions—I think we all work in a kind of a continuum. We try to make art, but whether we're aware of it or not, we're continuing what somebody else started, and for me, I keep seeing Joyce, you know, at the headwaters in your work.

GAINES: Right, yes, and like Turgenev, I guess the small chapters and the small books. I think he was my first great influence after reading his *Fathers and Sons*—when I was writing *Catherine Carmier.* But you draw from everybody. I'm drawing from Shakespeare. When I was writing that chapter when Raoul discovers that Catherine is running away with Jackson, you know, I was thinking about *King Lear.* He was just going mad, you know. Raoul is going mad when he realizes that his daughter and his life are running away from him. Writing *In My Father's House,* I had Greek tragedy in mind—the strong man falls, and he can't get up and all this sort of thing. That's why I had such a problem writing that book. You know, I'm drawing from all of these books I've read, things I've studied in college. I learned from all of that. It's not only one.

MG: Do you think that is true in your writing now, especially in writing *The Man Who Whipped Children* [Gaines's novel in progress]? Do you think you're drawing from different influences at this stage?

GAINES: Yes, I think so. I think that my voice—my particular voice—is the most dull and boring thing in the world. I have to draw from other people. I have my own story to tell, but I'm constantly getting into the voices of other characters. I don't wish to reach a point where I feel I cannot learn from others. I'm going to always try to learn from others. Like my brother, you know, who just lost his wife and less than two weeks later had to have his leg amputated. And I'd go in to cheer him up, and he was cheering *me* up all the time. My brother Lionel, you know, he's *funny*. He was telling me the funniest stories about the hospital and some of the people in the hospital.

MG: I agree that's one of the sources—in the oral tradition especially—the great storytellers like Lionel.

GAINES: Yes, he is a great storyteller. And he's still telling stories. He was telling me that the doctors told him that they were afraid they would have to take his leg off. And he told the doctor, "I'd rather be up here with one leg than to be down there with two."

MG: *Down* there!

DB: That's great.

GAINES: So I told him, I said, "Man, you sure are brave." I don't know what I'd do. I'd have to think about that for a week.

DB: And he could just rattle it off.

MG: And just the way he phrased it.

GAINES: His wife had just died a week or so before that. I said, damn, I know he's always been a braver man than I, but damn! What are you going to do?

MG: I love that story you told me about when he wanted to get out of the hospital—

GAINES: Right, they told him he would leave on Wednesday, and he said, "They better not crawfish on me, or they're going to see a one-leg man on the highway in his wheelchair." He said, "I'm getting on out of here." He had all those nurses and those doctors in that hospital laughing. He didn't care what he said. I wish I had his courage.

ALSO BY ERNEST J. GAINES

BLOODLINE

In these five stories, Gaines returns to the cane fields, sharecroppers' shacks, and decaying plantation houses of Louisiana. He introduces us to this world through the eyes of guileless children and wizened jailbirds, black tenants and white planters. He shows his characters eking out a living and making love, breaking apart and coming together. And on every page he captures the soul of a black community whose circumstances make even the slightest assertion of self-respect an act of majestic—and sometimes suicidal—heroism.

Fiction/0-679-78165-X

CATHERINE CARMIER

Catherine Carmier is a compelling love story set in a deceptively bucolic Louisiana countryside, where blacks, Cajuns, and whites maintain an uneasy coexistence. After living in San Francisco for ten years, Jackson returns home to his benefactor, Aunt Charlotte. Surrounded by family and old friends, he discovers that his bonds to them have been irreparably rent by his absence. In the midst of his alienation from those around him, he falls in love with Catherine Carmier, setting the stage for conflicts and confrontations that are complex, tortuous, and universal in their implications.

Fiction/0-679-73891-6

A GATHERING OF OLD MEN

"A sheriff is summoned to a sugarcane plantation, where he finds one young white woman, about eighteen old black men, and one dead Cajun farmer. The sheriff is sure he knows who killed the Cajun—although each of the men is toting a shotgun, only one of them could hit a barn door—but threats and slaps fail to change their stories. Each one claims guilt, and all but one promise to provoke a riot at the courthouse if the sheriff tries to make an arrest. In the meantime, they wait for a lynch mob that the dead man's father—like his son, a notorious brute—is sure to launch. . . . Before it is over, everyone involved has been surprised by something: the old men not least of all, by their first taste of power and pride" (*The New Yorker*).

Fiction/0-679-73890-8

IN MY FATHER'S HOUSE

In My Father's House is a compelling novel of a man brought to reckon with his buried past. In St. Adrienne, a small rural black community in Louisiana, Reverend Phillip Martin—a respected minister and civil rights leader, devoted husband and father, a man of strength and rectitude—comes face to face with the sins of his youth in the person of Robert X, a young, unkempt, vaguely sinister stranger who arrives in town for a mysterious meeting with the Reverend.

Fiction/0-679-72791-4

A LESSON BEFORE DYING

A Lesson Before Dying is set in a small Cajun community in the late 1940s. Jefferson, a young black man, is an unwitting party to a liquor store shootout in which three men are killed; the only survivor, he is convicted of murder and sentenced to death. Grant Wiggins, who left his hometown for the university, has returned to the plantation school to teach. Wiggins's aunt and Jefferson's godmother persuade him to visit Jefferson in his cell and impart his learning and pride to Jefferson before his death. In the end, the two men forge a bond as they both come to understand the simple heroism of resisting—and defying—the expected.

Fiction/0-375-70270-9

OF LOVE AND DUST

When young Marcus is bonded out of jail, where he has been awaiting his trial for murder, he is sent to the Hebert plantation to work in the fields. He treats the Cajun overseer, Sidney Bonbon, with supreme contempt, even as Bonbon works him nearly to death. Marcus takes his revenge by seducing Bonbon's black mistress, Pauline, and then his wife Louise. Jim Kelly, the tractor driver, watches the contest between the two men, knowing Marcus is doomed and hating him for disturbing the status quo. Grudgingly, however, Jim begins to admire the young man's spirit as the inevitable climactic showdown draws near.

Fiction/0-679-75248-X